WITHDRAWN

Race and Class

London, Chicago, Melbourne

Race and Class

Alex Callinicos

Race and Class / *Alex Callinicos*
Published January 1993
Bookmarks, 265 Seven Sisters Road, London N4 2DE
Bookmarks, PO Box 16085, Chicago, Il. 60616
Bookmarks, GPO Box 1473N, Melbourne 3001

ISBN 0 906224 83 7

Printed by Cox and Wyman Ltd, Reading

Bookmarks is linked to an international grouping of socialist organisations:
AUSTRALIA: **International Socialist Organisation**,
GPO Box 1473N, Melbourne 3001
BELGIUM: **Socialisme International**,
Rue Lovinfosse 60, 4030 Grevignée
BRITAIN: **Socialist Workers Party**,
PO Box 82, London E3 3LH
CANADA: **International Socialists**,
PO Box 339, Station E, Toronto, Ontario M6H 4E3
CYPRUS: **Workers Democracy**,
PO Box 7280, Nicosia, Cyprus
DENMARK: **Internationale Socialister**,
Ryesgade 8, 3, 8000, Århus C
FRANCE: **Socialisme International**,
BP 189, 75926 Paris, Cedex 19
GERMANY: **Sozialistische Arbeitersgruppe**,
Wolfsgangstrasse 81, W-6000, Frankfurt 1
GREECE: **Organosi Sosialistiki Epanastasi**,
PO Box 8161, 10010, Omonia, Athens
HOLLAND: **Groep Internationale Socialisten**,
PO Box 9720, 3506 GR Utrecht
IRELAND: **Socialist Workers Movement**,
PO Box 1648, Dublin 8
NORWAY: **Internasjonale Sosialister**,
Postboks 9226, Grønland 0134, Oslo
POLAND: **Solidarnosc Socjalistyczna**,
PO Box 12, 01-900 Warszawa 118
SOUTH AFRICA: **International Socialists of South Africa**,
PO Box 18530, Hillbrow 2038
UNITED STATES: **International Socialist Organisation**,
PO Box 16085, Chicago, Il. 60616

Contents

Alex Callinicos is a leading member of the Socialist Workers Party in Britain and the author of numerous books, including *The Revenge of History*, *Against Postmodernism*, *The Revolutionary Ideas of Karl Marx*, *Trotskyism* and *South Africa between Apartheid and Capitalism*.

Preface

THIS BOOK is a considerably revised and extended version of an article which first appeared in *International Socialism* journal. I am grateful to Duncan Blackie, Lindsey German, Chris Harman, Gary McFarlane, Kevin Ovenden, John Rees, Ahmed Shawki and Julie Waterson for their help in its writing.

The way in which racism can infiltrate ordinary language makes it important to pick the words one uses with care when writing about race. Thus I use the term 'black' in this book to refer to all those who are racially oppressed on the grounds of their colour. As the Black Power movement of the 1960s made clear, blackness is a political rather than a biological or cultural concept. Usage, however, varies from country to country. Thus in the United States 'black' tends to be used exclusively to refer to African-Americans, while in Britain it usually applies to Africans, Afro-Caribbeans and Asians alike. It should in any case be stressed that the analysis given here of the plight of blacks is broadly true of other racially oppressed groups, such as Hispanics in the US, Arabs in France and Turks in Germany.

Chapter 1

Introduction

RACISM REMAINS one of the main features of the advanced capitalist societies. It is institutionalised in the systematic discrimination which black people experience in jobs, housing and the education system, and the harassment they suffer at the hands of police and immigration authorities. Blacks are also the victims of racist violence, as the murders in recent years of Rolan Adams, Rohit Duggal and Stephen Lawrence in south east London, and Michael Griffiths and Yusuf Hawkins in New York bear witness

A striking development in European politics since the East European revolutions of 1989 has been the resurgence of racism, both in the unofficial form of the fascist and racist parties which have been able to make significant electoral gains recently (most notably in France, Germany and Belgium) and in the official form of the concerted attempts by European governments further to restrict immigration, most importantly by attacking the right to asylum. The more united European Community in which bourgeois politicians and even many socialists place their hopes will be Fortress Europe, its doors firmly closed to the impoverished masses of a Third World which most of the ex-Stalinist states seem in the process of joining.

As for the most powerful capitalist society on earth, the United States, a recent study by the academic Andrew Hacker argues:

> Black Americans are Americans, but they still subsist as aliens in the only land they know. Other groups may remain outside the mainstream—some religious sects, for example—but they do so voluntarily. In contrast, blacks must endure a segregation that is far from freely chosen. So America may be seen as two separate nations. Of course, there are places where the races mingle. Yet, in most significant respects, the separation is pervasive and penetrating. As a human and social division, it surpasses all others—even gender—in intensity and subordination.[1]

The great Los Angeles rebellion of April 1992—whose echoes were heard in other American cities as diverse as San Francisco, Las Vegas and Atlanta—showed how race and class together have the potential to blow apart the structures of US society.

The stark fact that the rich capitalist democracies are profoundly racist societies demands action to challenge and, if possible, to abolish racism. Plainly, any anti-racist strategy presupposes an analysis of the nature and causes of racism. The traditional liberal view, still very influential, treats racism primarily as a matter of *attitudes*: the problem is that whites are prejudiced against black people. The obvious solution would seem then to be educating whites out of their prejudices; such a diagnosis is implicit in the programme of Racism Awareness Training (RAT) which, developed in the US in the 1970s, was taken up by a number of Labour councils in Britain during the 1980s.[2] At the same time the old liberal goal of integrating black minorities into their Western 'host' societies tended to be replaced by the idea of multiculturalism. This involved conceiving society as a collection of ethnic groups each with its own irreducibly different culture; the aim was now a pluralistic arrangement based on the mutual understanding by the different groups of each others' cultures, involving, in particular, an appreciation by the white majority of the value of non-European traditions.[3]

More radical anti-racists, by contrast, see racism not as a matter of the ideas in people's heads, but of *oppression*, of systematic inequalities in power and life chances stemming from an exploitive social structure; the solution lies therefore in political struggle, in the liberation of black people from their oppression. But within the radical camp there are vital differences in analysis and strategy. Black nationalists tend to see racism as a state of affairs whose origins, structure and dynamic, while connected to those of the capitalist mode of production, cannot be reduced to them; black liberation, the nationalists conclude, can be achieved only by black people themselves organised separately from white anti-racists. Revolutionary Marxists, by contrast, regard racism as a product of capitalism which serves to reproduce this social system by dividing the working class; it can be abolished, therefore, only through a socialist revolution achieved by a united working class, one in which blacks and whites join together against their common exploiter.[4]

Chapter 2

Marxism: a European tradition?

THE DIFFERENCE between Marxism and black nationalism isn't always as starkly posed as this. Many black radicals have been influenced by versions of Marxism (usually some combination of Stalinism and academic Western Marxism). They draw on Marxist analyses of the slave trade and of imperialism, and argue that contemporary racism is of economic benefit to capitalism. Sometimes the kinship to Marxism seems very close.[5]

There are, however, definite limits to this overlap of Marxism and black nationalism. Black nationalist intellectuals tend to see Marxism as a Eurocentric tradition—a body of thought so deeply rooted in European culture that it is simply incapable of identifying with the plight and expressing the aspirations of the oppressed black masses, both in the Third World and in the advanced capitalist countries.

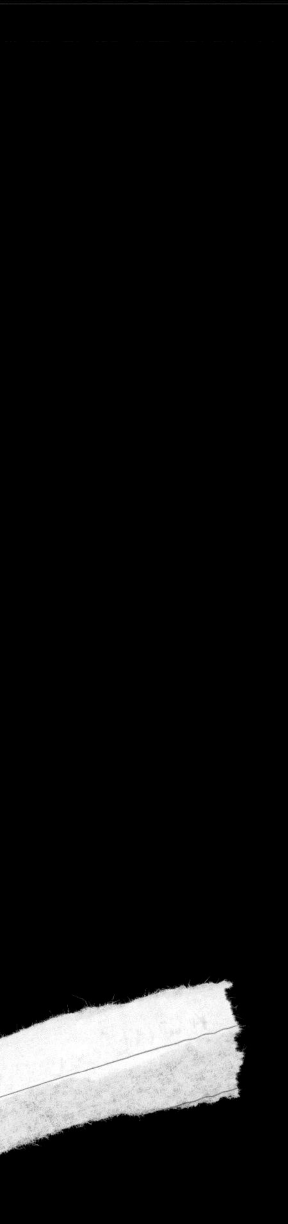

mention

The resulting conflict between Marxism and black nationalism is perhaps most systematically explored by Cedric Robinson, an American scholar associated with the Institute of Race Relations in London, in his book *Black Marxism*. Robinson's basic thesis is that Marxism is, in the very way in which its concepts are ordered, a Eurocentric ideology:

> at base, that is to say at its epistemological substratum, Marxism is a Western construction—a conceptualisation of human affairs and historical development which is emergent from the historical experiences of European peoples mediated, in turn, through their civilisation, their social orders, and their cultures.

Marxism, Robinson claims, isn't just European in its origins, but in 'its analytical presumptions, its historical perspectives, its points of view'. It consequently has failed to confront a 'recurring idea' in 'Western civilisation', namely racism and, in particular, the way in which 'racialism would inevitably permeate the social structures emergent from capitalism'. Twentieth century black radical intellectuals—Robinson traces the paths taken by three, WEB Du Bois, CLR James, and Richard Wright—have therefore had to work their way out of Marxism and rediscover an older tradition, 'the persistent and continuously evolving resistance of African peoples to oppression', for it is they, and not 'the European proletariat and its allies', which constitute the 'negation' of 'capitalist society'.[6]

The trouble is that Robinson's conception of the radical black tradition which he counterposes to Marxism verges on the mystical. 'The distinctions of political space and historical time have fallen away so that the making of one black collective identity suffuses nationalisms', he asserts, 'Harboured in the African Diaspora there is a single historical identity which is in opposition to the systemic privations of racial capitalism.' Robinson seems to be saying that all the struggles by black people against their oppression in both Africa and the New World have served to forge a shared identity, but when he comes to explain the nature of this identity Robinson descends ever deeper into obscurity, for example declaring that the black radical tradition's 'focus was on the structures of the mind', whatever this means.[7] The real differences between forms of struggle—the attempts by maroons to survive at the margins of the slave colonies of the New World, the Haitian Revolution and other slave risings, the resistance by African polities to European colonial expansion, the great urban risings by American blacks in the 1960s, the contemporary struggle against apartheid, not to speak of the actual conflicts among black people—say, between supporters of the African National Congress and Inkatha in South Africa—are all dissolved into a single vague abstract 'identity'.

The challenge posed by Robinson and his co-thinkers nevertheless remains. Can the classical Marxist tradition of Marx and Engels, Lenin and Trotsky, provide an analysis of racism capable of providing the basis of an effective strategy for black liberation? This little book is an attempt to meet that challenge.

What I shall try to show is that racism is a modern phenomenon. It's often claimed that racism is as old as human nature, the implication being that we can't get rid of it. On the contrary, racism as we know it today first developed in the seventeenth and eighteenth centuries in order to justify the systematic use of African slave labour in the great plantations of the New World which were central to the original emergence of capitalism as a world system. Racism, that is, was formed as part of the process through which capitalism became the dominant social and economic system. Its subsequent fortunes have been bound up with those of capitalism.

Thus racism today arises from the divisions that are fostered among different groups of workers whose competition on the job market is intensified by the fact that they often come from different parts of the world and are drawn together within the borders of the same state by capital's insatiable appetite for labour power. Racism therefore serves to set workers against each other, and to prevent them from effectively fighting against the bosses who exploit them all, irrespective of their colour or national origin.

Two very important political conclusions can be drawn from this analysis. The first is that racism operates against the interests of *all* workers, white and black alike. A divided working class harms even those workers who are not the direct victims of racism. Therefore a central component of any anti-racist strategy must be to win white workers to identify their interests with those of black people who suffer racial oppression. Black nationalists are therefore wrong when they dismiss the white working class as an irredeemable racist rabble. Secondly, the goal of anti-racist struggle must be the liberation of the oppressed as part of a broader battle against capitalism itself. Racism has grown up with capitalism and helps to sustain it; its abolition therefore depends on a socialist revolution that will break up the material structures with which it is bound up.

This is an analysis of racism which takes class as its starting point: racism underpins the domination of the capitalist class, and can only be overthrown by a united working class. There are many objections to such an analysis. Surely, for example, it goes against common sense to claim that white workers don't benefit from racism? Don't most blacks form an underclass which excludes them from the world of work dominated by whites? Won't racism survive a socialist revolution? These and other questions will be addressed in what follows. My aim, however, is less to provide a definitive answer to every question than to show that Marxism offers the best method for both understanding and fighting racism.

Chapter 3

Where does racism come from?

RACISM IS a historical novelty, characteristic of modern capitalist societies. This claim is central to the Marxist analysis of racism; it is, correspondingly, denied by many black nationalists. Cedric Robinson, for example, claims that racism is not a capitalist but a peculiarly European phenomenon: 'Racialism insinuated not only mediaeval, feudal and capitalist social structures, forms of property, and modes of production, but as well the very values and traditions of consciousness through which the peoples of these ages came to understand their worlds and their experiences.'[8] Similarly, the black American scholar Manning Marable argues that 'racism and patriarchy are both *pre-capitalist* in their social and ideological origin.'[9] The implication is that racism would survive the overthrow of capitalism, and that consequently a separate black movement is necessary to eradicate it.

To appreciate why this view is mistaken we must first consider the nature of racism. Racism exists where a group of people is discriminated against on the basis of characteristics which are held to be inherent in them as a group. Racism is often associated with a difference in the skin colour of the oppressors and the oppressed, but this is by no means a necessary condition of racism. Irish people were the victims of racism especially in nineteenth century Britain despite being as white as the 'natives'. Modern anti-semitism is another case of racism which is not based on colour differences. There is a sense in which difference in skin colour isn't even a sufficient condition for the existence of racism. Where it is involved it is as part of a complex of characteristics—for example, inferior intelligence, laziness, overactive sexuality, in the case of the traditional Western stereotype of Africans—which are imputed to the oppressed group and which serve to justify their oppression. It is the idea of some systematic set of differences between oppressor and oppressed, of which any visible physical differences are part, that is important rather than the physical differences themselves.

What confuses the matter is that classical racist ideology tends to highlight supposed physical differences between groups of people. The most theoretically articulated version of racist ideology is what Peter Fryer calls the 'pseudo-scientific mythology of race' that flourished in Britain (and indeed the rest of the developed capitalist world) between the 1840s and the 1940s. This held that humankind was divided into races each based on distinct biological characteristics and that the domination of the world by Western imperialism reflected the inherent superiority of the white races over the rest in the process of natural selection.[10]

Now the idea of biologically distinct races has no scientific basis:

> Of all human genetic variation known for enzymes and other proteins, where it has been possible to actually count up the frequencies of different forms of the genes and so get an objective estimate of genetic variation, 85 percent turns out to be between individuals within the same local population, tribe, or

> nation; a further 8 percent is between tribes or nations within a major 'race'; and the remaining 7 percent is between major 'races'. This means that the genetic variation between one Spaniard and another, or between one Masai and another, is 85 percent of all human genetic variation, while only 15 percent is accounted for by breaking up people into groups... Any use of racial categories must take its justifications from some other source than biology. The remarkable feature of human evolution and history has been the very small degree of divergence between geographical populations as compared with genetic variation among individuals.[11]

Racial differences are *invented*: that is, they emerge as part of a historically specific relationship of oppression in order to justify the existence of that relationship. So what is the historical peculiarity of racism as a form of oppression? In the first instance, it is that the characteristics which justify discrimination are held to be *inherent* in the oppressed group. A victim of racism can't change herself and thus avoid oppression; black people, for example, can't change their colour. This represents an important difference between, for example, racial and religious oppression, since one solution for someone persecuted on religious grounds is to change their faith.

There is thus no escape from racial oppression for members of the subordinate 'race'. Now this form of oppression is peculiar to capitalist societies. It must be distinguished from a pervasive feature of pre-capitalist societies, namely prejudices against strangers. Most people before the advent of industrial capitalism were peasants living in small rural communities. Poor communications meant that contact with anywhere outside an extremely narrow radius was rare. The result was often an intense, even suffocating, involvement in each others' lives within the peasant community, combined with deep ignorance and suspicion of strangers. What the sociologist Zygmunt Bauman calls 'heterophobia' (resentment of the different), is not the same as modern racism: 'In a world that boasts the unprecedented ability to improve human conditions by reorganising human affairs on a rational basis, racism manifests the conviction that a certain category of human beings cannot be incorporated into the rational order, whatever the effort.'[12]

What is striking about the slave and feudal societies of pre-capitalist Europe is, contrary to the claims of Robinson and Marable, the absence of ideologies and practices which excluded and subordinated a particular group on the grounds of their inherent inferiority. The slave societies of classical Greece and Rome do not seem to have relied on racism to justify the wholesale use of chattel slaves to provide the ruling class with its surplus product. The black American historian Frank M Snowden Jnr writes: 'Social intercourse [between black and white] did not give rise among the Greeks and Romans to the colour prejudices of certain later Western societies. The Greeks and Romans developed no theories of white superiority.'[13] The most striking instance of the absence of racism based on colour in classical antiquity is provided by the case of Septimius Severus, Roman Emperor from AD 193 to 211, who was almost certainly black. One of the main characteristics of Roman rule was the effort to incorporate local aristocracies into an imperial ruling class sharing a culture which fused the Greek and Roman traditions.

Another case in point is provided by Martin Bernal's celebrated book *Black Athena*. This has had an enormous impact among black radicals because it seeks to show that classical Greece—which still occupies a sanctified position within Western culture as the origin of European civilisation—was an offshoot of more advanced societies in Africa and Asia. Plainly it would be a powerful blow to Western racism if Bernal's historical thesis could be proved right. There are, however, difficulties with the thesis which needn't detain us here.[14] Of more direct relevance is the fact that Bernal sees himself reviving what he calls the 'Ancient Model', according to which Greek culture was a result of colonisation from Egypt, and from Phoenicia (on the coast of what is now Syria and Lebanon). He argues that this theory was only displaced in the late eighteenth century as a result of the rise of racism:

> For 18th and 19th century Romantics it was simply

> intolerable for Greece, which was seen not merely as epitome of Europe but also as its pure childhood, to have been the result of the mixture of native Europeans and colonising Africans and Semites. Therefore the Ancient Model had to be overthrown and replaced by something more acceptable.[15]

As Bernal constantly reiterates, 'the "Ancient Model" was the conventional view among Greeks in the Classical and Hellenistic ages.'[16] Its most important source is Herodotus's *Histories*, which sought to explain the Persian Wars at the beginning of the fifth century BC by exploring the Greeks' relations with Asia and Africa. Despite the fact that the climax of his book is devoted to the struggle between the Greek city states and the Persian Empire, Herodotus constantly stresses the Greeks' dependence on African and Asian influences. For example, he argues that Greek religion had its origins in Egypt: his respect for this far more ancient civilisation is evident.[17] A similar attitude informs Herodotus's treatment of Persia itself. As Arnoldo Momigliano puts it, 'Herodotus respects the Persians and considers them capable of thinking like Greeks... his thinking is basically committed to the mutual understanding of Greeks and Persians.'[18] Whether or not the Ancient Model offers, as Bernal claims, an accurate account of the origins of classical Greece, the belief, expressed most systematically by Herodotus, in the Greeks' historical debt to their African and Asian neighbours is an indication of the absence of any ideology of racial exclusivity and superiority in antiquity.

In the feudal societies which emerged in Western Europe after the fall of Rome, the ruling classes identified themselves as followers of a particular religion, Christianity. Feudal Europe conceived itself as Christendom, at war with the adherents of the rival faith of Islam. Judith Herrin observes:

> As the ancient world collapsed, faith rather than imperial rule became the feature that identified the universe, what Christians called the *oikoumene*, and Muslims, *Dar al Islam*. Religion had fused the political, social, and cultural into self-contained systems, separated by their differences of faith.[19]

The Mediterranean world (and its extensions in northern and central Europe and in central Asia) thus became polarised between two rival civilisations, Islam and Christendom, whose conflict spanned ten centuries, from the Arab conquest of much of the eastern Roman Empire soon after the death of Islam's founder Muhammed in 632 until the second siege of Vienna in 1683. But despite the ferocity of this struggle it was not a racial struggle. Conversions from one faith to the other sometimes occurred. During the Crusades Christian and Muslim rulers often struck alliances, and at the height of the Ottoman threat to Christendom in the sixteenth century the King of France tended to support the Turkish Sultan in his struggle with the Habsburg rulers of Spain as a way of weakening a dangerous European rival.

Adherents to faiths other than the dominant one were often discriminated against or persecuted in various ways: the most notable instances in the case of mediaeval Christendom were perhaps the widespread massacres of Jews at the time of the First Crusade at the end of the eleventh century and the extermination of the Cathars of Languedoc at the beginning of the thirteenth century. Nevertheless religious persecution of this kind was not the same as racial oppression. This is perhaps best brought out by the case of the Jews. What Hannah Arendt calls 'the assumption of an eternal anti-semitism', according to which 'outbursts need no special explanation because they are natural consequences of an eternal problem', is quite widespread.[20] On this view, the Holocaust takes its place as merely the latest case of 2,000 years of anti-semitism. But, as Zygmunt Bauman points out, while in pre-modern Europe Jews were in a peculiarly vulnerable position because of their status as religious outsiders, this 'did not on the whole prevent their accommodation into the prevailing social order... In a society divided into estates or castes the Jews were just one estate or caste among many. The individual Jew was defined by the caste to which he belonged, and by the specific privileges or burdens the caste enjoyed or bore. But the same applied to every other member of the same society.'[21] Modern anti-semitism developed in the nineteenth century against the background of the collapse of this hierarchical order of estates, and treated the Jew no longer as a religious outsider but as a member of a biologically inferior race. It was the emergence of racial anti-semitism which made the Nazi 'Final Solution' conceivable in ideological terms. In Arendt's words, 'Jews had been able to escape from Judaism [religion] into conversion; from Jewishness [race] there was no escape.'[22]

By the end of the nineteenth century, Jews were no longer a religious minority, with their place—albeit a subordinate and vulnerable one—within the prevailing social order. In the turbulent, warring and polarised societies of modern Europe they had become marked out ideologically as the main scapegoat for these antagonisms. The Jews acquired this label as a result of the racial ideology which, as we shall see, had been constructed as a justification for European domination of the rest of the world. The Nazi's attempt to exterminate them therefore was not the latest expression of what one author calls 'the oldest hatred' but a consequence of the profound tensions at the heart of modern capitalism.

Chapter 4

Slavery and the development of capitalism

RACISM AS we know it today developed during a key phase in the development of capitalism as the dominant mode of production on a global scale—the establishment during the seventeenth and eighteenth centuries of colonial plantations in the New World using slave labour imported from Africa to produce consumer goods such as tobacco and sugar and industrial inputs such as cotton for the world market. Peter Fryer has traced its development in Britain: 'Racism emerged in the oral tradition in Barbados in the seventeenth century and crystallised in print in Britain in the eighteenth, as the ideology of the plantocracy, the class of sugar-planters and slave-merchants that dominated England's Caribbean colonies.'[23] The most influential statement of this ideology was provided by Edward Long in his *Histo-*

ry of Jamaica (1774), but already in 1753 the great Scottish philosopher David Hume, one of the giants of the eighteenth century Enlightenment, had declared: 'I am apt to suspect the negroes, and in general all the other species of men (for there are four or five different kinds) to be naturally inferior to the whites.'[24]

The development of what Robin Blackburn calls 'systemic slavery' in the plantations of North America and the West Indies, requiring the import of some 6 million African captives in the eighteenth century alone, is one of capitalism's greatest crimes.[25] It is, however, a common argument that it was the prior existence of racism which led to the exploitation of African slaves. This interpretation was challenged by Eric Williams in his classic study of the subject: 'Slavery was not born of racism: rather, racism was the consequence of slavery. Unfree labour in the New World was brown, white, black, and yellow; Catholic, Protestant and pagan.'[26]

Indeed, the plantation economies initially relied on unfree *white* labour in the shape of indentured servants, who agreed to work for a particular master on a servile basis for three to five years, in exchange for free passage from Europe. According to Blackburn:

> more than half the white emigrants to colonial North America arrived as indentured servants; the French and British Caribbean also absorbed tens of thousands of these tied labourers, who could be purchased more cheaply than slaves. Altogether some 350,000 servants were shipped to the British colonies up to the 1770s.[27]

Barbara Fields argues that the tobacco plantations of colonial Virginia 'rested primarily on the backs of English indentured servants, not African slaves', until the late seventeenth century:

> Indentured servants served longer terms in Virginia than their English counterparts and enjoyed less dignity and less protection in law and custom. They could be bought and sold like livestock, kidnapped, stolen, put up as stakes in card games, and awarded—even before their arrival in America—to the victors in lawsuits. Greedy magnates (if

the term is not redundant) stinted the servants' food and cheated them out of their freedom dues, and often out of their freedom itself, when they had served their time. Servants were beaten, maimed, and even killed with impunity.[28]

As Fields observes, 'the only degradation' white servants 'were spared was perpetual enslavement along with their issue in perpetuity'. This was their chief disadvantage to plantation owners concerned to secure a stable, long term labour supply to meet the growing demand for colonial products. But, Fields argues, it was not their colour which prevented the indentured servants' full scale enslavement, but the limits on landowners' power imposed by 'centuries of day-to-day contest, overt and covert, armed and unarmed, peaceable and forcible,' between exploiters and exploited in England:

> To have degraded the servants into slaves *en masse* would have driven the continuing struggle up several notches, a dangerous undertaking considering that the servants were well-armed, that they outnumbered their masters, and that the Indians could easily take advantage of the inevitably resulting warfare among the enemy. Moreover, the enslavement of already arrived immigrants, once news of it reached England, would have threatened the sources of future immigration. Even the greediest and most short-sighted profiteer could foresee disaster in any such policy.[29]

The solution to the planters' problems of labour supply was provided from the 1680s onwards by 'the importation of African labourers in larger and larger numbers', which 'made it possible to maintain a sufficient corps of plantation labourers without building up an explosive charge of armed Englishmen resentful at being denied the rights of Englishmen and disposing of the material and political resources to make their resentment felt'.[30] Racism developed in the context created by the development of the 'systemic slavery' of the New World: the idea that Africans were (in Hume's words) 'naturally inferior' to whites justified denying them 'the rights of

Englishmen' and enslaving them.

But this raises another question. Why was it necessary to justify slavery in the first place? This may seem like an odd question, until we consider the other main historical example of a society based on slave labour, classical antiquity. Ellen Wood observes:

> Some people may be surprised to learn that in ancient Greece and Rome, despite the almost universal acceptance of slavery, the idea that slavery was justified by natural inequalities among human beings never caught on. The one notable exception, Aristotle's conception of natural slavery, never gained currency. The more common view seems to have been that slavery was a convention, though a useful one, which was justifiable simply on the grounds of its usefulness. In fact, it was even conceded that this useful institution was *contrary to nature*. Such a view appears not only in Greek philosophy but was even recognised in Roman law. It has even been suggested that slavery was the only case in Roman law where there was an acknowledged conflict between the *ius gentium*, the conventional law of nations, and the *ius naturale*, the law of nature.[31]

Why did the ideologues of Greece and Rome find it unnecessary to come up with any elaborate justification of what they acknowledged to be an 'unnatural' institution? To answer this question we must keep in mind one of the basic features of pre-capitalist class societies namely their reliance on what Marx called 'extra-economic force'. Ancient slavery and mediaeval feudalism both rested on the exploitation of unfree labour. The slave was reduced to the status of a chattel, a speaking tool (*instrumentum vocale*), as the Romans put it. As such, the slave was totally subject to the physical power of the master, who could beat, rape, torture, and even kill him or her. This extreme subordination of one group of people to another presupposed the military power of the Greek city states and the Roman empire, which provided them with a ready supply of slaves. The feudal peasant, though typically enjoying greater rights and control over a patch of land, was subject to the military and judicial power of the lord. This power was used to compel the peasant to work for the lord, by providing him with forced labour services, either working a part of the week on the lord's own land or supplying him with a portion of the peasant's crop.[32]

The nature of exploitation in these societies was reflected in their hierarchical organisation and the division of the population into legally unequal groups—citizen and slave in classical antiquity (and indeed the citizens themselves were divided between rich and poor), the estates of mediaeval Europe. Inequality of a visible, systematic, legally entrenched kind was the norm in pre-capitalist societies. Their ideologues took it for granted, and tended to depict society as based on a division of labour in which even the most humble had their allocated role. The ancient Greek philosopher Plato's famous dialogue *The Republic*, with its hierarchy of Guardians, Warriors and Labourers, is the classic Western version of this ideology. Another example is quoted by the great mediaeval Arab philosopher, Ibn Khaldûn:

> The world is a garden the fence of which is the dynasty. The dynasty is an authority through which life is given to proper behaviour. Proper behaviour is a policy directed by the ruler. The ruler is an institution supported by the soldiers. The soldiers are helpers, who are maintained by money. Money is sustenance brought together by the subjects. The subjects are servants protected by justice. Justice is something familiar, and, through it, the world persists. The world is a garden...[33]

In such hierarchical societies slavery was merely one of a spectrum of unequal statuses, requiring no special explanation. Not so in capitalist society. For the capitalist mode of production rests on the exploitation of free wage labour. The wage labourer is, Marx says, 'free in a double sense, free from the old relations of clientship, bondage and servitude, and secondly free of all belongings and possessions, and of every objective, material form, *free of all property*.'[34] It is not the workers' legal and political subordination to the exploiter, but their separation from the means of production, and the resulting economic compulsion to sell their only productive resource, labour power, that is the basis of capitalist exploitation.

The worker and capitalist confront each other in the labour market as legal equals. Workers are perfectly free not to sell their labour power: it is only the fact that the alternative is starvation or the dole which leads them to do so. Hence the labour market is, as Marx puts it, 'a very Eden of the innate rights of man', 'the exclusive realm of Freedom, Equality, Property, and Bentham'. It is only in 'the hidden abode of production' that exploitation takes place.[35]

This contrast between the formal equality and the real inequality of capitalist and worker is a fundamental feature of bourgeois society, reflected in many aspects of its development. The great bourgeois revolutions, which swept away the obstacles to the dominance of the capitalist mode of production, mobilised the masses under the banner of freedom and equality. 'The poorest he that is in England has a life to live as the greatest he, and therefore... every man that is to live under a government ought first by his own consent to put himself under that government,' said Colonel Rainsborough in the Putney Debates of 1647. 'We hold these truths to be self-evident, that all men are created equal, that they are endowed by their Creator with certain unalienable rights, that among these are life, liberty, and the pursuit of happiness', the American Declaration of Independence of 1776 proclaims. And the Great French Revolution of 1789 was waged under the banner of *Liberté, Égalité, Fraternité*.

And yet the paradox was that capitalism, whose domination involves the exploitation of free wage labour, benefited enormously during a critical phase in its development from colonial slavery. This relationship continued well into the era of the Industrial Revolution as the textile factories of northern England imported their main raw material from the slave plantations of the American South. Capitalism's reliance on slave labour became an anomaly requiring explanation. It was in this context that the idea that blacks were subhuman, and therefore did not demand the equal respect that was increasingly acknowledged as the right of human beings, began to take hold.

Barbara Fields argues that 'racial ideology' took hold especially among the 'white yeomanry' in the southern US—

the small farmers and artisans who, representing nearly two thirds of the population of the Old South, largely did not own slaves and sought to assert their claim to political and economic independence of the planters:

> Racial ideology supplied the means of explaining slavery to people whose terrain was a republic founded on radical doctrines of liberty and natural rights; and, more important, a republic in which those doctrines seemed to represent accurately the world in which all but a minority lived. Only when the denial of liberty became an anomaly apparent even to the least observant and reflective members of Euro-American society did ideology systematically explain the anomaly.[36]

Similarly, Peter Fryer shows how racism emerged in eighteenth century Britain 'as a largely defensive ideology—the weapon of a class whose wealth, way of life, and power were under mounting attack'.[37] Racist ideologues such as Long wrote to defend the West Indian planters from the growing pressures to abolish, not just the slave trade, but the very institution of slavery itself. Yet racist ideology survived abolition, and indeed received further theoretical elaboration during the nineteenth century in the shape of the pseudo-scientific biology of races which drew on a vulgarised version of Darwin's theory of natural selection. This reflected the fact that the anomaly which had given rise to racism in the first place continued to exist in another form, the domination of the world by a handful of European (or, in the case of the US and Russia, Europeanised) powers. This state of affairs was justified by the idea that the biological constitution of Asians and Africans suited them to rule by the white 'races', whose duty it was to govern the world in the interests of their subjects. The classic statement of this view is Rudyard Kipling's poem 'The White Man's Burden', written in 1898 as an appeal to the US, then just beginning its career as an imperial power, to:

> Take up the White Man's burden—
> Send forth the best ye breed—
> Go bind your sons to exile
> To serve your captives' need;

To wait in heavy harness
On fluttered folk and wild—
Your new-caught, sullen peoples,
Half devil and half child.[38]

Chapter 5

Racism in contemporary capitalism

RACISM IS thus a creature of slavery and empire. It developed in order to justify the denial to the colonial oppressed of the equal rights that capitalism tended to promise all of humankind. The argument so far therefore establishes a historical connection between racism and capitalism. But what about racism today? Simply to halt the analysis at this point would leave contemporary racism as some sort of hangover from the past which had somehow managed to survive the abolition of slavery and the collapse of the colonial empires. This, at any rate, seems to be Peter Fryer's view: 'Long after the material conditions that originally gave rise to racist ideology had ceased to exist, these dead ideas went on gripping the minds of the living. They led to various kinds of racist behaviour on the part of many white people in Britain, including white people in authority.'[39] This analysis, asserting as it does that racism no longer has any material foundations, implies that the main task of anti-racists, among white people at any rate, is to change attitudes, presumably through some process of education. It is mistaken, however: the material conditions of modern capitalism continue to give rise to racism.

Let's note, in the first place, a change in racist ideology. Martin Barker is one of a number of writers to have noted the emergence of what he calls the 'new racism', which highlights, not the biological superiority of some races to others, but the cultural differences among 'ethnic' groups.[40] The ideologues of the Tory right in Britain, from Enoch Powell to Norman Tebbit, have used the idea that the cultural differences between European and non-European peoples make it impossible for them to live together in the same society to justify tighter immigration controls and even (in Powell's case) the repatriation of black people. But the most notorious example of this variant of racism is Margaret Thatcher's remark during a television interview on *World in Action* on 30 January 1978: 'People are really afraid that this country might be rather swamped by people with a different culture.'

How big a change does the 'new racism' represent, and what caused its emergence? To start with the latter question, as we have seen, the idea that humankind is divided into races with different biological constitutions is no longer scientifically respectable. It is, moreover, positively disreputable morally and politically because of the use the Nazis made of it. The Holocaust made biological racism in its nineteenth century form stink—hence the shift from biology to culture, and from race to ethnicity.

The change must not, however, be overstated. In the first place, biological racism is still around, for example, in sociobiology's attempts to explain social inequalities in biological terms and in the idea that American blacks' poor scores in IQ tests reflect genetic differences between them and whites.[41] Secondly, the idea that blacks are naturally inferior to whites is still very much part of popular racism, though it tends to use the idea of cultural differences as a respectable cloak. Often certain apparently innocent words used in public pronouncements represent a tacit coded appeal to cruder racist attitudes. Thatcher's use of the word 'swamp' is a case in point: it's surely no accident that the police operation, involving large scale harassment of blacks, which sparked the riot in Brixton, south London, in April 1981 was called 'Swamp 81'.

Thirdly, the 'cultural' or 'ethnic identities' which have taken the place of 'race' in polite discussion tend to involve the same kind of crude stereotypes characteristic of old fashioned racism.[42] 'Ethnicity' or 'culture' is conceived as a fate from which those it embraces cannot escape. Although acknowledged as a product of (usually caricatured) history, it is no longer amenable to further change by human action: it has become effectively part of nature. At most those in one 'ethnic' prison can try to understand other people's prisons (multiculturalism), or they can exchange prisons, as Tebbit demanded of black people when he proposed his 'cricket test' (blacks could only be regarded as British if they supported England in cricket matches with teams from the West Indies, India and Pakistan), which amounted to insisting that, to be British they must, in effect, break all connections with the countries from which they or their ancestors emigrated and assimilate to the dominant culture—a test which he assumed most would fail.[43]

Modern racism, with its rhetoric of cultural difference and usually tacit appeal to older notions of natural inferiority, in any case arises in the conditions of industrial capitalism. Capitalism in its fully developed form rests on the exploitation of free wage labour. But the working class which sells its labour power to capital is internally composite in two ways. First of all, the technical division of labour requires a workforce with different kinds of skill; one of the functions of the labour market is to meet this requirement, variations in wage rates serving as a means of allocating different kinds of labour power. Secondly, to secure an adequate supply of labour capitalists are often forced to reach beyond the borders of the state in question, drawing towards them workers of different national origin. Eric Hobsbawm has pointed out that 'the middle of the nineteenth century marks the beginning of the greatest migration of peoples in history', starting with the great flood of European immigrants to the US, and to a lesser extent South America, Australasia and South Africa.[44] The most spectacular result is the US itself, the proverbial 'nation of immigrants', its working class entirely formed from successive waves of immigration. But there are many other cases, ranging from the role of Irish migrant labour in Victorian Britain to the large scale use of Polish labourers by Prussian landowners in the late nineteenth century. Reliance on immigrant labour has proved to be a structural feature of advanced capitalism in the second half of the twentieth century. By the early 1970s there were nearly 11 million immigrants in Western Europe, who had come from southern Europe or former colonies during the boom of the 1950s and 1960s.[45] And even during the crisis-ridden 1970s and 1980s the US economy continued to suck in a vast new immigration from Latin America and east Asia.

Capitalists employ immigrant workers because of the economic benefits they bring: they contribute to the flexibility of labour supply, are often unable to refuse employment in low paid, dirty jobs frequently involving shiftwork, and, since the costs of their upbringing have been met in their country of origin, make, through the taxes they pay, a net contribution to the reproduction of labour power in the 'host' country.[46] But, more than that, the existence of a working class composed of 'natives' and immigrants (or, in the case of countries like the US, largely of less and more recent immigrants) makes possible the division of that class on racial lines, particularly if differences in national origin at least partially correspond to different positions in the technical division of labour (for example, between craft workers and unskilled labourers).

Marx grasped the way in which racial divisions between 'native' and immigrant workers could weaken the working class, as he showed in his famous letter of 9 April 1870 to Meyer and Vogt. Here Marx seeks to explain why the Irish struggle for self determination was a vital issue for the British working class:

And most important of all! Every industrial and com-

> mercial centre in England possesses a working class *divided* into two hostile camps, English proletarians and Irish proletarians. The ordinary English worker hates the Irish worker as a competitor who lowers his standard of life. In relation to the Irish worker he feels himself a member of the *ruling* nation and so turns himself into a tool of the aristocrats and capitalists of his country *against Ireland*, thus strengthening their domination *over himself*. He cherishes religious, social, and national prejudices against the Irish worker. His attitude towards him is much the same as that of the 'poor whites' to the 'niggers' in the former slave states of the USA. The Irishman pays him back with interest in his own money. He sees in the English worker at once the accomplice and stupid tool of the *English rule in Ireland*.
>
> This antagonism is artificially kept alive and intensified by the press, the pulpit, the comic papers, in short by all the means at the disposal of the ruling classes. This *antagonism* is the *secret of the impotence of the English working class*, despite its organisation. It is the secret by which the capitalist class maintains its power. And that class is fully aware of it.[47]

In this remarkable passage Marx sketches out the outline of a materialist explanation of racism in modern capitalism. We can take him as identifying three main conditions of existence of racism:

i) *Economic competition between workers* ('the ordinary English worker hates the Irish worker as a competitor who lowers his standard of life'). A particular pattern of capital accumulation implies a specific distribution of labour which is reflected in the labour market by different wage rates. Particularly in periods of capital restructuring when labour is deskilled, capitalists (being what they are) are tempted to replace established skilled workers with cheaper and less skilled workers. If the two groups of workers have different national origins, and probably therefore also different languages and traditions, the potential exists for the development of racial antagonisms among the two groups of workers. This is a pattern which has repeated itself often enough in the history of the American working class.[48] The racial divisions involved need not, however, arise from the attempt by skilled workers to defend their position. On a number of occasions in the nineteenth and early twentieth centuries American blacks were driven out of the skilled niches they had managed to attain by white workers—for example, by unskilled Irish immigrants in the period before the civil war.[49]

ii) *The appeal of racist ideology to white workers* ('the ordinary English worker... feels himself a member of the ruling nation'). The mere fact of economic competition between different groups of workers is not enough to explain the development of racial antagonisms. Why do racist ideas appeal to white workers? One answer is that it reflects their economic interest in racial oppression: white workers, in other words, benefit materially from racism. This explanation is, I argue below, mistaken. The basis of another, better, explanation is sketched out by WEB Du Bois in his great work *Black Reconstruction in America* (1935). Du Bois was trying to account for the division among black and white workers after the defeat of Radical Reconstruction—the efforts by an alliance of ex-slaves and white radicals to uproot racism in the American South after the civil war. He argues that:

> the [Marxist] theory of labouring class unity... failed to work in the South... because the theory of race was supplemented by a carefully planned and slowly evolved method, which drove such a wedge between the white and black workers that there probably are not today in the world two groups of workers with practically identical interests who hate and fear each other so deeply and persistently and who are kept so far apart that neither sees anything of common interest.
>
> It must be remembered that the white group of labourers, while they received a low wage, were compensated for by a sort of public and psychological wage. They were given public deference and titles of courtesy because they were white. They were admitted freely with all classes of white people to public functions, public

> parks, and public schools. The police were drawn from their ranks, and the courts, dependent upon their votes, treated then with leniency as to encourage lawlessness. Their vote selected public officials, and while this had small effect upon the economic situation, it had great effect upon their personal treatment and the deference shown them. White schoolhouses were the best in the community, and conspicuously placed, and they cost anywhere from twice to ten times as much per capita as the coloured schools. The newspapers specialised in news that flattered the poor whites and almost utterly ignored the Negro except in crime and ridicule.
>
> On the other hand, in the same way, the Negro was subject to public insult; was afraid of mobs; was liable to the jibes of children and the unreasoning fears of white women; and compelled almost continuously to submit to various badges of inferiority. The result of this was that the wages of both classes could be kept low, the whites fearing to be supplanted by Negro labour, the Negroes always being threatened by the substitution of white labour.[50]

Du Bois is concerned here with a peculiarly extreme case of racism—the American South in the era of Jim Crow, so powerfully depicted by Richard Wright in books like *Uncle Tom's Children.* But his argument permits a more general extension. It has two elements. First, racism meant that 'two groups of workers with practically identical interests' were divided, so that 'the wages of both classes could be kept low'; Du Bois thus argues against the black nationalists like Cedric Robinson who want to claim him for their own, that white workers don't have an interest in the oppression of blacks (a view emphatically shared by another contributor to Robinson's supposed 'black radical tradition', CLR James).[51] Secondly, white workers received, in compensation for their low wages, 'a sort of public and psychological wage' deriving from their membership of what Marx calls 'the *ruling* nation'.

Marx in fact provides the means to understand how this process of compensation works in a famous passage in the 1843 Introduction to his *Contribution to the Critique of Hegel's*

Philosophy of Right: 'Religious distress is at the same time the *expression* of real distress and also the *protest* against real distress. Religion is the sigh of the oppressed creature, the heart of a heartless world, just as it is the spirit of spiritless conditions. It is the *opium* of the people'.[52] Religious beliefs are thus not just an invention foisted on the masses by a clerical conspiracy, as the philosophers of the Enlightenment had argued; they are accepted because they provide an imaginary solution of real contradictions. Religion offers solace for the ills of this world in a heavenly world beyond the grave. Its power lies in its recognition of the existence of suffering and oppression, even though its solution is a false one. Marx here uncovers one of the mechanisms at work in ideologies in general, including racist ideology. Racism offers white workers the comfort of believing themselves part of the dominant group; it also provides, in times of crisis, a ready made scapegoat, in the shape of the oppressed group.

Racism thus gives white workers a particular identity, and one moreover which unites them with white capitalists. We have here, then, a case of the kind of 'imagined community' discussed by Benedict Anderson in his influential analysis of nationalism. The nation, he argues, is 'an imagined political community': in particular, 'regardless of the actual inequality and exploitation that may prevail in each, the nation is always conceived as a deep horizontal comradeship'.[53]

The crucial phase in the development of popular nationalism in the advanced capitalist countries came in the late nineteenth century, as part of the process through which the European ruling classes sought to incorporate newly enfranchised, increasingly organised workers within the same community.[54] Against a background of growing competition among the imperialist powers, workers were encouraged to identify their interests with those of 'their' ruling classes in these rivalries. It was in this same period that the pseudo-scientific biology of race received its most developed formulation: it served not merely to justify Western imperialist domination of the world, but also to sanctify the conflicts among the great powers as one aspect of the struggle for survival among the races. Racism buttressed nationalism, leading workers to see themselves as members, like their exploiters, of the higher races which were fighting each other for supremacy of the world. Of course nationalism in general is not the same as racism—many nationalists, particularly those involved in struggles for colonial liberation, have combined an identification with their own nations with a sincere belief in the equality of peoples, but imperialist nationalism provides a breeding ground where, in the right conditions, racism can grow.

iii) *The efforts of the capitalist class to establish and maintain racial divisions among workers* ('this antagonism is kept artificially alive by the press, the pulpit, the comic papers, in short by all the means at the disposal of the ruling classes'). Marx makes it clear that racism is in the interests of capital, calling it 'the secret by which the capitalist class maintains its power' and stressing that 'that class is fully aware of it'. This sounds a bit as if Marx is saying that racism is just the result of a capitalist conspiracy. This is not so. As we have seen, there is an objective economic context of racial divisions, namely capital's constantly changing demands for different kinds of labour which can often only be met through immigration. We have also seen that racism offers for workers of the oppressing 'race' the imaginary compensation for the exploitation they suffer of belonging to the '*ruling* nation'. It is, moreover, an objective fact about capitalism that racism helps keep capitalism going by dividing and therefore weakening the working class. The adage, 'Divide and rule', is an ancient piece of ruling class wisdom, coined by the Roman Emperor Tiberius in the first century AD. Capitalist domination does not occur automatically—it must actively be organised. One way of doing this is through promoting racism. It happens all the time: George Bush cynically used racism to help win the 1988 presidential election in the US. Capitalism isn't just a bosses' conspiracy, but capitalists do quite often resort to racism to divide the working class.[55]

Chapter 6

Black and white workers

RACISM, THEN, helps to keep capitalism going. It is thus in the interests of the capitalist class. But what about the working class? Perhaps the single most important difference between Marxists and black nationalists is that the latter believe that white workers materially benefit from racism. The other side of this belief tends to be the idea of a black movement which transcends class divisions. This is theorised in various ways. Cedric Robinson argues that the agency of revolutionary change is not the industrial working class but the 'black radical tradition' articulating the 'black collective identity' forged by centuries of resistance. 'The experimentation with Western political inventories of change, specifically nationalism and class struggle, is coming to a close. Black radicalism is transcending those traditions in order to adhere to its own authority.'[56] Paul Gilroy takes Marxists to task for positing 'a complete discontinuity... between the interests of the black *petit bourgeois* and working-class black settlers on the basis of their objectively contradictory class position'. 'Dogmatism' of this kind ignores 'the construction of the Black Community as a complex and inclusive collectivity with a distinctive political language'.[57] A Sivanandan is committed to a much more robust form of class analysis, yet his primary focus is on 'the new underclass of homeworkers and sweatshop workers, casual and part time workers, *ad hoc* and temporary workers, thrown up by the putting out system in retailing, the flexi-system in manufacturing, and the hire and fire system in the expanding service sector' rather than the entire working class, white as well as black.[58]

Denying that white workers have an interest in fighting racism is often justified by resorting to the idea that they form a privileged labour aristocracy benefiting from imperialist super-profits extracted from Third World toilers. As originally formulated independently by Lenin and Du Bois during the First World War, the theory of the labour aristocracy was an attempt to explain reformism by arguing that it reflected the material interests of a *layer* of the Western working class.[59] In the hands of the black nationalists, however, it becomes the idea that all workers in the advanced economies share in the fruits of imperialism. Thus Ron Ramdin declares that 'the exploitation and degradation of the colonial working class was an indispensable requirement in maintaining the standard of living of the British working class.'[60]

The idea is, however, completely untenable. In the first place, the theory of the labour aristocracy is an extremely poor guide to the behaviour of the Western working class during the heyday of classical imperialism in the late nineteenth and early twentieth centuries. Aside from the flaws in its economic arguments, the theory does not explain why the most plausible candidate for the title of 'labour aristocrats', the skilled metal workers, formed in all the main European industrial centres—Petrograd, Berlin, Turin, Sheffield, Glasgow—the vanguard of the great surge of working class revolt at the end of the First World War.[61]

Secondly, the idea that the entire Western working class now forms a labour aristocracy tends by be underpinned by the theory that there is a process of 'unequal exchange' going on between North and South: the result is that Western workers live off resources extracted from the peoples of the Third World. The main evidence used to support this theory is the fact that wage levels are higher in the advanced capitalist countries than they are in the Third World. Proponents of unequal exchange appeal to Marx's theory of exploitation to support their analysis. But this theory isn't primarily about how badly off particular groups of workers are. It's about the *relationship* between the wages workers receive, which reflect the costs to the capitalist of reproducing their labour power, and the amount of surplus value they produce over and above these costs, which represent the capitalist's profits.

How exploited a worker is depends, not on his or her absolute standard of living, but on how much surplus value he or she produces relative to his or her wages. A highly paid worker may well be more exploited than a low paid worker because the former produces, relative to his wages, a larger amount of surplus value than the latter does. There is indeed reason believe that the generally higher wages paid to Western workers reflect the greater costs of their reproduction; but the expenditure in particularly on education and training which forms part of these costs creates a more highly skilled workforce which is therefore more productive and more exploited than its Third World counterparts.[62]

There is in any case a simple test of the proposition, essential to the labour aristocracy and unequal exchange theories, that Third World workers are more exploited than Western workers. If this were true one would expect a constant flow of capital from the rich to the poor countries in search of the higher profits to be gained in the latter. In fact, according to the World Bank, between 1965 and 1983 two thirds of all foreign direct investment went to the advanced economies, and the rest to a handful of Newly Industrialising Countries (NICs). The debt crisis of the 1980s actually made the situation worse: capital flow from North to South almost dried up, while Third World capital flight and debt repayments meant there was, for much of the decade, a net transfer of financial resources from the poor to the rich countries.[63]

Writers such as Sivanandan are absolutely right to highlight and denounce the poverty and degradation to which imperialism condemn the masses of the Third World. But he relies on a doubly mistaken economic theory when he claims that 'the brunt of exploitation has shifted to the underdeveloped countries of the Third World', where 'capital does not need to pay peripheral labour a living wage to reproduce itself'.[64] This alleged development has passed Western capitalists by who continue, as we have seen, to concentrate their investments in their own heartlands of Western Europe, North America and Japan. Moreover, while Sivanandan is right to point to the way in which capitalists in rich and poor countries alike often seek to increase their profits simply by squeezing the existing workforce, by cutting wages and lengthening working hours, he ignores the changes wrought by the partial industrialisation of the Third World. The emergence of the NICs of East Asia and Latin America has rested on the formation of relatively highly educated and skilled working classes which have in recent years been able to organise and to extract political and social reforms from their exploiters. The classic case is that of South Africa where, amid the appalling suffering and oppression caused by apartheid, the black working class has been able to build, in the shape of the Congress of South African Trade Unions, the most powerful labour movement in African history.[65] The bourgeoisie continues to create its own gravedigger in the shape of the working class. The new workers' movements of the Third World share a common interest with their Western brothers and sisters, black and white alike, in the overthrow of capitalism.

The fundamental reason why Marxists argue that racism is not in the interests of white workers is that, by dividing the working class, it weakens white as well as black workers. This proposition and the rival hypothesis that white workers gain from racism have been tested for the United States by the Marxist sociologist Al Szymanski. Szymanski sought to compare the situation of white and black workers in the 50 states of the Union. He found, first, that 'the higher black earnings relative to white, the higher white earnings relative to other whites' elsewhere in the US. This relationship—white workers were better off the narrower the gap between their wages and those of blacks—was stronger in states where at least 12 percent of the population were 'Third World' (ie black, Hispanic, Asian and native American), 'ie those states where economic discrimination against Third World people is able to have a significant economic effect on white earnings'.

Szymanski found, secondly, that 'the higher the population of Third World people in a state's population, the *more* inequality there is among whites'. He concluded that 'the relatively poor white workers lose disproportionately from economic discrimination against Third World people compared with the better paid whites.' Thus 'white workers appear to actually lose economically from racial discrimination. These results appear to support the Marxist theory of the relationship between economic discrimination and white gain.' Szymanski found, thirdly, some evidence to support the hypothesis that 'the more intense racial discrimination is, the lower are the white earnings because of the intermediate variable of working-class solidarity—in other words, racism economically disadvantages white workers because it weakens trade union organisation by undermining the solidarity of black and white workers.'[66]

Szymanski's study suggests that racism is contrary to the interests of white workers, even when these interests are understood in the narrowest material terms. This is one facet of a much broader claim, namely that racism helps to keep capitalism going and thereby perpetuates the exploitation of white and black workers alike. White workers accept racist ideas not because it is in their interests to do so, but because of the way in which labour market competition among different groups of workers is worked up, by the conscious and unconscious efforts of the capitalists, into full scale racial divisions. At most what white workers receive is the imaginary solace of being members of the superior race, which helps to blind them to where their real interests lie. This analysis offers a cue to how the hold of racism on white workers can be broken—through the class struggles which pit them against the bosses and unite them with their black brothers and sisters.

White liberals and black nationalists alike nevertheless believe that most blacks form a separate 'underclass' set apart from the mass of white workers. This kind of view of where blacks fit into the class structure is often backed up by fashionable theories put forward by ex-Marxists (or, as they often like to describe themselves, 'post-Marxists') to the effect that capitalism has radically changed, dissolving the old class antagonism between capital and labour and replacing it with a much more fragmented society. Sivanandan is a fierce critic of such theories, so it is surprising that he accept one of their main elements, the idea that a new 'post-Fordist' economy has emerged based on the destruction of the mass production industries and the working class these rested on. He merely argues that the effect of these changes is to shift the locus of resistance to the new 'underclass' which now bears the brunt of exploitation—'peripheral workers, home workers, *ad hoc* workers, casual, temporary, part-time workers—all the bits and pieces of the working class that the new productive forces have dispersed and dissipated their strength'.[67] This is, since Sivanandan still wants to fight capitalism, a remarkably pessimistic analysis. It is, however, a completely mistaken one. As I have shown elsewhere, the whole idea of a new 'post-Fordist' phase of 'flexible accumulation' which no longer rests on mass industrial production is completely untenable.[68]

Ideas of an underclass in particular involve a gross exaggeration of limited trends. Thus the proportion of the employed and self employed working part time rose in Britain from 21 percent in 1984 to 22 percent in 1991 (the proportion of women working part time actually fell slightly in the same period). The proportion of those in temporary jobs was 5.7 percent in 1984, 5.8 percent in 1991.[69] Moreover, the concept of the underclass is wholly misleading in suggesting that black people typically occupy a marginal economic position in the advance countries.

An ambitious Marxist survey of contemporary class structure, conducted in the United States in 1980 under the supervision of Erik Olin Wright found that no less than 74.5 percent of blacks were workers, as opposed to 49.7 percent of

UNEMPLOYMENT RATES BY ETHNIC ORIGIN AND SEX, GREAT BRITAIN, SPRING 1991 (%)

	All persons	Men	Women
All persons of working age	8.3	9.1	7.3
Whites	8	9	7
Ethnic minority groups	15	16	14
of which:			
West Indian/Guyanese	15	18	12
Indian	12	12	11
Pakistani/Bangladeshi	25	25	24
All other ethnic origins	14	14	14

Source: M Naylor and E Purdie, 'Results of the 1991 Labour Force Survey', *Employment Gazette*, April 1992, Table 20

whites. Interestingly, it found that 15.4 percent of all blacks and 21.4 percent of black men were skilled workers (the equivalent figure for all whites was 12.4 percent and for white men 16.7 percent.)[70]

Other evidence from the US helps to fill out this picture. Levels of unionisation are actually higher among black than among white workers. 24.4 percent of male black workers belong to unions, but only 18.8 percent of their white counterparts. Similarly 18 percent of black women workers are union members, compared to 11.7 percent of white women workers. Blacks are more likely to be unemployed than whites: in the 1960s the black unemployment rate was, on average, 2.06 times of the white, in the 1970s 2.01 times, in the 1980s 2.37 times. Nevertheless, these figures need to be set in proportion: at its highest level in the past generation, in 1983, the black unemployment rate reached 19.5 percent. Terrible though this is (and the levels of black unemployment were and are much higher among particular groups in particular localities—for example, young men in South Central Los Angeles), the fact remains that the bulk of blacks were in employment rather than, as underclass theorists would have it, excluded from economic life.[71]

No comparably rigorous study has been made of the British class structure, but the unemployment figures in the 1991 Labour Force Survey (see table) are indicative. The average rate of unemployment among blacks was 15 percent, almost twice that among whites (8 percent). This is clear evidence of the effects of racism: blacks are more likely than whites to suffer unemployment. Nevertheless the overwhelming majority of blacks are in employment, as wage labourers, part of the same working class as their white brothers and sisters.

This argument shouldn't be misunderstood. There are throughout the inner cities of the advanced capitalist world, black neighbourhoods with terrible concentrations of unemployment, poverty and casual sweated labour. Here exploitation and oppression mutually reinforce each other, with appalling consequences. But these realities do not mean that all blacks have an economically marginal status. Most, as we have seen, are wage labourers. Moreover, their fellow white workers do not have an interest in the oppression of blacks. On the contrary, this oppression helps to keep the working class divided and weak. White workers therefore has as strong an interest in getting rid of racism as black people have.

Chapter 7

Community and class

WE HAVE been considering arguments about the material situation and interests of black and white workers. Black nationalists tend to see the black community as the chief agent of the struggle against racism. For Sivanandan it is the 'communities of resistance' forged by the black 'underclass' out of struggle which bear the main burden of fighting capital today.[72] Culture is accorded a central role in the creation of such communities. Paul Gilroy argues that 'collective identities, spoken through "race", community and locality are, for all their spontaneity, powerful means to coordinate action and create solidarity. The constructed "traditional" culture becomes a means... to articulate personal autonomy with collective empowerment'.[73]

This stress on culture is far from wholly mistaken. The attempts, for example, to develop an 'Afrocentric' history which recovers the achievements of pre-colonial African societies and the centuries of heroic struggle by black people against Western imperialism and racism can be an important source of black pride infusing contemporary political movements with strength: the real value of Cedric Robinson's *Black Marxism*, for example, lies in the contribution it makes to this process of recovery. But to base the struggle against racism on the idea of a black community united by a culture of resistance carries with it great dangers. Probably the most obvious is that blacks form a minority of the population in the advanced capitalist countries—12 percent in the US, 5 percent in Britain. Central to the defeat of the greatest and most heroic of all black nationalist movements, the Black Power movement which emerged in the US from the great ghetto risings of the 1960s, was the failure of even its most advanced wing, represented by Malcolm X and the Black Panthers, to link the struggle for black liberation with that of white workers against their exploitation. This allowed the ruling class to isolate and ultimately to destroy the black radicals, many of whose best leaders were murdered or jailed.[74]

A strategic focus on the black *community*, secondly, conceals the class antagonisms within this 'community'. Again the US provides the best illustration. Manning Marable, himself an influential black radical theorist, observes: 'The net result of affirmative action and civil rights initiatives was to expand the potential base of the African-American middle class... By 1989, one out of seven African-American families had incomes exceeding 50,000 dollars annually, compared to less than 22,000 dollars for the average black household.' The process of class differentiation among blacks underlies the rise of the black politicians who now largely manage America's cities. Marable confesses: 'Most of us have not anticipated an ideological shift among many African-American or Latino politicians, using racial solidarity to ensure minority voter loyalty, but gradually embracing more moderate to conservative public policy positions, especially on economic issues.'[75] As the Los Angeles rebellion showed, black politicians have become the district commissioners of a ruling class that is still predominantly white, defending a racist system against the very people who elected them.

Thirdly, theorists like Gilroy who place the main emphasis on the development of a culture of resistance ignore the way in which culture can divide, rather than unite, black people. The recovery of, or return to, a tradition may appeal only to particular groups of black people. Many Asians, for example, may feel that Afrocentric history has nothing to offer them. The renewed interest in Islam among many young British Asians may cut them off from many other black people, let alone from white workers. The Newham Monitoring Project and the Campaign against Racism and Fascism make a relevant point when discussing the anti-racist policies of the Greater London Council and other left Labour led London councils in the early 1980s:

> Instead of welding those groups previously excluded from the local state to form a movement for socialism, local authority funding policies actually placed the groups in a competitive relationship with each other. In the black community, this accentuated the differences between Asians, Africans and Caribbeans, and even divided the groups among themselves. Over the previous decade at least, there had been a significant political dimension to black struggles, but council funding tended to promote the more cultural and less political organisations. Furthermore, the focus on 'ethnicity' within council funding policy tended to promote religious and cultural organisations over campaigning ones.[76]

These tensions are one example of the rise of what is sometimes called 'identity politics' in the 1980s. In the absence of large scale struggles against oppression, the oppressed themselves tended to fragment into smaller groups, each tending to highlight their different 'identities', the particularity of *their* oppression compared to those of others—blacks of African origin versus Asians, black women versus gentile white women versus Jewish white women, gays versus lesbians versus bisexuals. This kind of fragmentation can only weaken any real struggle against the system which produces all the different forms of oppression. Of course, appeals to culture need not have this kind of effect. Real cultures of resistance can be forged which include and unite rather than exclude and divide. But then why should such a culture be confined to black people? Why shouldn't it unite blacks and whites in a common struggle in the way in which Rock Against Racism sought to in the late 1970s? Indeed, Mike Davis, who calls the Los Angeles rising the 'first modern multi-ethnic riot' in the US, argues that rap has helped to create 'a broad interface between black youth culture and Latino youth culture' in Los Angeles.[77]

Chapter 8

Los Angeles: class rebellion, not race riot

THE LOS ANGELES rebellion repays closer analysis, not simply because of its scale—the greatest urban upheaval in the US since the New York Draft Riots of July 1863, leading to 53 deaths and $1 billion worth of damage—but because it demonstrates how class rather than race is the fundamental faultline in American society.[78]

There is, of course, an obvious sense in which race was central to the rebellion. After all, it was sparked off on 29 April 1992 by the acquittal by a white jury of four white police officers videotaped beating up a black motorist, Rodney King. The affair highlighted the racial injustices endemic in US society. Nor is it an accident that at the heart of the rising was South Central Los Angeles, an area economically devastated by the run-down of the heavy industries on which local blacks had depended for jobs, traumatised by the fighting between gangs over the drug trade which had helped fill the resulting vacuum, and at the fulcrum of the Los Angeles Police Department's 'Operation HAMMER'—a series of vast paramilitary police sweeps through the ghetto in which thousands of youths were arrested on trivial charges.[79]

Nevertheless the Latino poet Luis Rodriguez is right to insist: 'Although "race" continues to be rammed down our throats, the issue here is class.'[80]

This can be seen in a number of ways. In the first place, the rebellion was *multi-ethnic* in character. Willie Brown, a leading black California Democrat and the speaker of the state assembly, acknowledged that 'the violence was not contained in the inner city; it spread to outlying and upscale neighbourhoods ... For the first time in American history, many of the demonstrations, and much of the violence and crime, especially the looting, was multi-racial—blacks, whites, Hispanics and Asians were all involved.'[81] Of the first 5,000 people arrested in the riot 52 percent were Latinos, 10 percent were whites, and only 38 percent were blacks.[82]

Underlying the multi-ethnic character of the rebellion was the double impact of Reaganomics—the economic policies of Reagan and Bush in the 1980s, which sought systematically to transfer wealth and income from rich to poor, leaving real wages to fall (inflation-adjusted weekly income per worker fell from $366 in 1972 to $312 in, 1977)—and of the major recession which set in in 1990, hitting the sometime boom economy of California particularly hard.[83]

Class didn't simply unite working class blacks with their counterparts of other races; it also divided them from the black middle class involved in managing LA and other big American cities. The mayor, Tom Bradley, the incoming police chief, Willie Williams, and the chairman of the US Joint Chiefs of Staff, General Colin Powell, on whose orders federal troops were deployed to quell the rising, were all black. The fact that New York, a racial cauldron in recent years, didn't explode—despite a panic-stricken exodus from Manhattan on 1 May 1992 prompted by fears that the rioting was about to spread there from LA—had much to do with the intervention of Mayor David Dinkins, in alliance with more radical black politicians like the Rev. Al Sharpton.

Yet much of the media coverage of the LA rebellion focused on the confrontation between the looters and Korean shopkeepers. This conflict could easily be used to reinforce the image—already encouraged by some of the most influential representations of the US in the 1980s such as Tom Wolfe's novel *The Bonfire of the Vanities* and the films of Spike Lee—of America as a society of warring ethnic groups.

Media treatment of the plight of the Korean merchants involved massive distortion. In the first place, the conflict was one which pitted them less against blacks than against the mass of LA's working poor. As Peter Kwong points out, '[t]he worst damage to Korean property ... did not occur in the African-American neighbourhood of South Central LA—only 9 percent of South Korean businesses in LA are located there. The heaviest loss occurred north of South Central, in Koreatown, which is inhabited mostly by poor Latino immigrants.'[84]

Moreover, the South Korean merchants occupy a specific location within the class structure of Los Angeles. Kwong explains:

> Anxious to escape from political instability and the high rate of unemployment at home, Korean professionals came in droves in the 1970s. They arrived with education, personal savings, military training (no one is allowed to emigrate from South Korea without first serving two years in the armed forces) and a willingness to work hard. These self-selected capitalists saw South LA as their stepping stone to the American Dream. They believed they would follow in the steps of those who had started earlier, have already 'made it' and now park their Mercedes beside homes built near affluent white neighbourhoods. After a time, they would build up enough money to move their businesses out of the ghettoes into more profitable white areas.
>
> Korean businesses in South LA—mainly groceries, liquor stores and swap meet stands—were perfectly suited for the needs of the system. The ghetto may be poor, but that doesn't mean there isn't any money to be made there.

> These new entrepreneurs provided valuable retail access to the ghetto for corporations like Brown Forman distilleries, R.J. Reynolds, General Foods and Coca Cola. They also provided the main economic activity in impoverished neighbourhoods and supplied essential merchandise to areas long abandoned by earlier, often Jewish-owned, businesses. Best of all, they did this without putting whites at risk. During the long American recession, as the major corporations laid off employees, small businesses have become the new chief source of new jobs, and many have been started by Asian immigrants. Some 38 percent of the retail outlets in LA County are Korean-owned, and Korean-American businesses in LA proper actually grew by 27 percent in the past two years. The cohesiveness of the community gives them a slight advantage in acquiring seed money—but not because, as some people in the neighbourhood believe, they have been favoured by white banks. Most Korean-Americans attain their capital in one of two ways: Either they labour at more than one job for up to 16 hours a day ... or they participate in a community savings club known as a *kye*. In a *kye*, perhaps a few dozen families chip in between $500 and $1000 annually; each year, one (decided by lot) gets that year's receipts to start a business.[85]

The Korean merchants are not the chief exploiters of the black and Latino poor. The slum lords who make vast profits out of rack-rents in the Latino neighbourhoods north of South Central LA, for example, are predominantly Anglo. But Asian shopkeepers are the only visible, directly accessible representatives of the system responsible for the poverty and degradation suffered by the mass of blacks and Latinos. Mike Davis calls them 'the lightning rod for the accumulated grievances of the Latino and black poor'.[86] Specific grievances also helped to make the Korean merchants targets—such as complaints of overcharging, the shooting of Latasha Harlins, a 15 year old black girl, because of a dispute with a Korean grocer over a $1.79 bottle of orange juice. Davis suggests that the celebrated black gangs, the Crips and the Bloods, who struck a truce three days before the rebellion began on 29 April, may have targeted the Korean stores in South Central LA, where 90 percent were destroyed in the first two days, as part of a conscious political strategy:

> I saw graffiti in South Central that advocated 'Day one: burn them out. Day two: we rebuild'. The only national leader whom most Crips and Bloods seem to take seriously is Louis Farrakhan, and his goal of black economic self-determination is broadly embraced ... At the Inglewood gang summit, which took place May 5, there were repeated references to a renaissance of black capitalism out of the ashes of Korean businesses. 'After all,' an ex-Crip told me later, 'we didn't burn out our community, just their stores.'[87]

The conflict between Korean merchants and black and Latino poor thus represented a displacement of the fundamental class antagonism away from the real source of the problem, the big corporations, US and foreign, which dominate the Southern Californian economy, onto a social layer which is only the middle man between capital and the working masses. As Manning Marable put it,

> [b]lack young people need to understand that it is not the Korean-American merchant who denies capital for investment in the black community, controls the banks and financial institutions or commits police brutality against blacks and Latinos. There may be legitimate complaints between the two groups. But such misdirected anger makes a unified response to race and class oppression virtually impossible.[88]

The issue is of significance far beyond Los Angeles. The large scale immigration of the past generation has produced inner city neighbourhoods throughout the advanced capitalist world where poor working class people of different ethnic backgrounds live side by side. Often particular ethnic groups occupy a particular niche in the labour market; sometimes members of a specific group take on the middle man role of the Korean merchants in LA (for example, Asian shopkeepers in many British inner cities). These circumstances create the potential for inter-ethnic conflict *among* the oppressed. Such conflict diverts fire away from the main enemy. But only a strategy which takes as its starting point class rather than race can provide the basis for the necessary unity of the oppressed.

Chapter 9

Racism and class struggle

THE LIMITATIONS of the LA rebellion reflect in large part the fact that, unlike the great ghetto risings of the 1960s, which represented a radicalisation of the existing movement for civil rights in the South, it came out of the blue, as Lee Sustar puts it, 'after an extremely conservative period'. He calls the 1992 rising 'an angry but pre-political rejection of the system'.[89] This doesn't alter the distinctiveness of the rebellion—the fact that, unlike the earlier risings, Harlem in 1964, Watts in 1965, Newark and Detroit in 1967, it crossed ethnic boundaries. In this respect LA's closest parallel is provided by the 1981 riots in many British inner cities. As Chris Harman noted at the time, though the British riots were usually sparked off by police racism, in '*virtually all*' of them 'there has been significant white involvement alongside blacks, and the involvement has not just been of white leftists, but of white working-class youth'.[90] Of those arrested in the riots, 67 percent were white, 20 percent West Indians and Africans, 5 percent Asians.[91] Like LA these were *class rebellions*, not race riots. They brought together black and white youth rebelling against a common experience of unemployment as well as protesting about specific grievances, such as police harassment, which particularly affected blacks.

These risings are part of a long history largely ignored by black radicals, that of working class struggles which brought together blacks and whites. One of the great achievements of Peter Fryer's superb and moving history of black people in Britain is its reconstruction of the role played by black radicals such as the Spencean William Davidson and the Chartist William Cuffay in the great revolutionary workers' movements of the early nineteenth century. Their participation in these struggles reflects the fact that the demand for the abolition of slavery in the British Empire, finally achieved in the 1830s, had as its main source of mass support the working class radicals who linked the struggle for black emancipation to that against oligarchy in Britain itself.[92]

Every great surge of mass workers' organisation in the United States has brought together black and white workers across the racial barriers. The Civil War saw America's greatest genuine race riot in New York in July 1863, when Irish immigrant workers protesting against the draft ran amok, killing 105 people, most of them blacks. But Radical Reconstruction—the efforts by the left wing of the Republican Party in the late 1860s to achieve genuine racial equality in the defeated Southern states—had as its mass base an alliance of freed black slaves and white small farmers and artisans uniting against the common enemy—the big plantation owners—and often demanding radical measures of land redistribution.[93]

The defeat of Reconstruction, which made possible the establishment in the South of the Jim Crow regime effectively denying blacks even legal equality until the Civil Rights movement of the 1960s, reflected the ruling class's concern that they needed to unite to face a new foe, the working class emerging in the industrial cities of the North. But even in the

Jim Crow era, every big workers' movement broke through the racial divide. The Knights of Labor had 700,000 members at its highpoint in 1886, 60,000 of them black. The great demonstrations on 1 May 1886, 'the first May Day in labour history', when 340,000 workers marched throughout the US to demand the eight hour day, brought black and white workers together onto the streets. Even the American Federation of Labor, which, unlike the Knights, concentrated on building craft unions of highly paid, overwhelmingly white, skilled workers, sought in its early years to organise blacks. The New Orleans General Strike of November 1892 brought out 25,000 black and white workers for four days under the leadership of the AF of L. Philip Foner comments:

> The outstanding feature of the strike was its great demonstration of interracial solidarity in action. Thousands of workers in the Deep South had shown that they could unite in a common struggle, black and white, skilled and unskilled, and that they could stay united despite the efforts of employers and their agents to divide them by appeals to anti-Negro prejudice.[94]

There have been many other episodes of interracial working class unity. Their importance is that, even if they were sometimes short lived, that they show that the level of class struggle is the decisive factor in determining the intensity of racism. Generally speaking, the higher the level of class struggle, the greater workers' militancy, confidence and self organisation, the wider the layers of the class involved in any particular movement, the weaker the hold of racism on them.

The London dockers are a case in point. Notoriously in April 1968 they went on strike for a day and marched on the Houses of Parliament in support of Enoch Powell's 'rivers of blood' speech calling for an end to black immigration. The dockers' action reflected the rundown of their industry under a Labour government which did nothing to defend their interests. In despair and anger they looked to Powell instead. By contrast, in July 1972 the dockers, relying now on their own shop stewards' organisation, inflicted a decisive defeat on the Tory Industrial Relations Act when they forced the release of the Pentonville Five. The confidence this victory instilled in the dockers strengthened support for more generalised class politics. Five years later, on 11 July 1977, the Royal Docks Shop Stewards' banner headed a mass picket of 5,000 overwhelmingly white trade unionists in support of the predominantly Asian workforce at Grunwicks in west London. The London dockers were largely resistant to the surge of fascism which swept Britain in the late 1970s.

There is, this example suggests, an inverse relationship between the level of class struggle and the intensity of racism. The crucial factor underlying this relationship is workers' self confidence. When the class is engaging successfully in battles with the bosses, then white workers are more likely to place their confidence in workers' self organisation to defend their interests, and to see themselves as part of the same class as their black brothers and sisters. By contrast, when the workers' movement is on the defensive and the employers are generally able to impose their will, then workers are much less likely to look towards class-based collective organisation and action to solve their problems. Racism can, in these circumstances, increase its hold on white workers, both because of the psychological compensations it seems to promise, and because it offers a diagnosis of their situation that focuses their sentiments on a visible scapegoat, black people.

This analysis can be illustrated by an interesting study of Newham in east London by the Newham Monitoring Project and the Campaign against Racism and Fascism. It documents the growth of racism in the borough during the 1970s. In the October 1974 general election the main Nazi group, the National Front, won the votes of 5,000 Newham residents, the largest NF vote in the country. According to a leading black activist in the area, Unmesh Desai, in 1980, 'anywhere east of Liverpool Street—and this is very difficult for people to comprehend now—was regarded as a no go area for black people.' The spread of racism in Newham took place against the background of the rundown of local industry—between 1966 and 1972, 45 percent of the 40,000 jobs in Canning Town were lost and only one in three replaced—and the failure of the Labour Party, which controlled the borough council, to offer any effective alternative:

> Newham, by the mid-1970s, had become one of the most neglected and deprived areas in the country. According to *New Society* (23 October 1975), it had the largest number of houses without bath or inside lavatory in London; the highest perinatal mortality rate (that is, still-births and deaths in the first week) and the highest percentage of mentally ill in the country. Only one in 40 schoolchildren went to university (the national figure was three times as high) and only one in ten received any form of further education (the national figure was almost one in four)... The general poverty and decline were aggravated by the way power was concentrated in the hands of a few individual councillors and council officers sought to manage social problems (and no more so than in the area of housing) by playing one group off against another.[95]

Leading Labour Party members indeed expressed openly racist attitudes: 'at a local Labour Party ward meeting, the former mayor of Newham (a local magistrate) started talking about the "coons", how they smelt, how he couldn't stand the smell of their cooking and how, if he had his own way, he would send them all back to where they came from.' It was in this climate that 'a substantial section of the white working class turned its electoral support away from the Labour Party to the NF. The latter might not be able to provide new houses and jobs or to alleviate the material conditions, but its message of white pride spoke to a psychological need.'[96]

Newham in the 1970s illustrates on a micro scale the process involved in the rise of the National Front in France during the 1980s. There a social democratic government presided over levels of unemployment higher over the decade than those in Thatcherite Britain and responded to the growth of racism by tightening up immigration restrictions; it is hardly surprising that millions of disillusioned working class voters deserted the parties of the reformist left, the Socialists and Communists, for Jean Marie Le Pen. These examples highlight the fact that rises in the level of racism are not, as is sometimes believed, an automatic consequence of deteriorating economic conditions. Working class people's experience of economic crisis is mediated by the role played by their political and industrial organisations. The failure of reformist organisations to mount an effective struggle against rising unemployment and falling living standards is often critical in laying workers open to racist ideas.

The subjective factor, the conscious attempt by political organisations to influence the course of history, can also play a decisive role in combating the spread of racism. The divergent experiences of Britain and France in the 1980s bear this out. The Newham study (published in 1991) reports: 'Ten years ago, Asian and Afro-Caribbean people across the whole of Newham, both north and south, were experiencing similar levels of racial harassment. But throughout the 1980s, a series of self-defence campaigns radically altered the climate in the north.' The study, while stressing the importance of the defence campaigns initiated by black people themselves—for example, after the 1980 murder of Alchtar Ali Baig by fascist skinheads—also acknowledges the role played by white anti-racists, for example, of the Labour left wingers who were able to reverse some of the council's most obnoxious racist practices (such as demanding that black people produce passports before their housing applications could be considered) and were responsible for Newham in 1984 becoming the first local authority to evict a white family for racial harassment. Reflecting on the experience of the Newham Monitoring Project, Unmesh Desai noted:

> another lesson we learned in those early days was that it was not white individuals who were the problem but white society as a whole. Anti-racism has also to speak to the problems of the white working class, who we have to live cheek by jowl with, and can't get away from.[97]

These developments in Newham were part of a nationwide process, one of whose main features was the precipitate decline of the NF and other fascist organisations at the end of the 1970s. This serious defeat for the far right in Britain was a direct consequence of the emergence of a mass anti-fascist movement, the Anti Nazi League, launched by the Socialist Workers Party and Labour left wingers in 1978. Yet the ANL has often been attacked by black nationalists. Paul Gilroy, for example, claims that 'the ANL deliberately sought to summon and manipulate a form of nationalism and patriotism as part of its broad anti-fascist drive', concentrating in its propaganda on the charge that 'the British Nazis were merely sham patriots'. Moreover, 'being "Anti Nazi" located the problem posed by the growth of racism in Britain exclusively at the level of a small and eccentric, though violent, band of neo-fascists.'[98] This indictment can be contested at a number of levels. In the first place, ANL propaganda focused, not on the Nazis' lack of patriotism, but on the fact that they were *Nazis*, active supporters of a political ideology which had led to the Holocaust. If there was a historical image to which the ANL appealed, it wasn't Britain's 'Finest Hour' in 1940, as Gilroy contends, but Auschwitz: hence its main slogan, 'Never again!'

At the same time, the ANL was based on a united front of social democrats and revolutionary socialists with differing analyses of racism and strategies of change. Labour ANL supporters, given their general commitment to British nationalism, did sometimes attack the Nazis' lack of patriotism. We in the SWP certainly did not. Nor did we isolate the struggle against fascism from broader questions of racism. For example, at the first ANL carnival in May 1978 an SWP pamphlet called *The Case against Immigration Controls* sold heavily; SWP activists made clear their opposition to immigration controls at ANL conferences. It is of the nature of a united front that it brings together divergent political forces which are prepared to work together around a single issue, in this case combating the Nazis. Focusing in this way on the fascists wasn't a retreat from the more general struggle against racism; on the contrary, it was essential to the conduct of that struggle at the time.

The growth of the NF and other Nazi organisations of course reflected a much more deep seated racism institutionalised in British society and pandered to by the main parties. But the rise of the NF (which one commentator predicted, in 1977, would soon overtake the Liberals as the third main party),[99] if unhindered, would have promoted a qualitative increase in the level of racism, allowing the Nazis to entrench themselves in many working class areas where they could draw on white popular support to attack black people with impunity and demand the implementation of even more racist policies by local authorities and central government. We can see this dynamic at work in France, where the official racism of the state and the main capitalist parties feeds off and also reinforces the popular racism stoked up by the Nazis. The ANL, by targeting and mobilising against the Nazis, stopped this dynamic in its tracks, and thereby helped to prevent a further intensification in the level of racism.

Perhaps the last word on the subject should go to Darcus Howe, one of Britain's best known black radicals. Paul Foot reports his 'brilliant and moving tribute' to David Widgery, one of the founders of Rock Against Racism and the ANL, at a meeting organised by the SWP in Widgery's memory in December 1992:

> Darcus Howe said he had fathered five children in Britain. The first four had grown up angry, fighting forever against the racism all around them. The fifth child, he said, had grown up 'black at ease'. Darcus attributed her 'space' to the Anti Nazi League in general and to David Widgery in particular. It is difficult to imaged a more marvellous epitaph.[100]

Chapter 10

Socialist revolution and black liberation

THE DEFEAT inflicted on British fascism at the end of the 1970s is no reason for complacency. Racism is inherent in capitalist society, and the conditions promoting it are constantly being recreated by the system's crisis. But the contrast between the British case and that of France since 1981 is instructive. It suggests that the failure of the French far left—which includes a number of sizeable and long established organisations—to build an anti-fascist movement comparable to the ANL is a major factor in the growth of the National Front. This in turn highlights the role which revolutionary socialists can play in the struggle against racism. They can do so at two levels. First, revolutionaries should be involved in the battles which develop around different aspects of racism—not just (or often primarily) against the Nazis, but against tighter immigration restrictions, attacks on the right of asylum, the deportations of individuals, police brutality, racial attacks. This active commitment to the struggle against racism in all its aspects includes support for black people when they organise against their oppression and when they take their grievances onto the streets, to challenge the racist state.

Fighting racism, however, depends on understanding its causes. This is essential if the hold of racism on white workers is to be broken. Racism, as we have seen, appeals to white workers because it offers an imaginary solution to the real problems—poverty, unemployment, exploitation—they confront. Therefore, the direct struggle against racism must be linked to agitation around social and economic issues which shows that racism *isn't* the solution, that the class struggle, uniting workers of all colours and ethnic backgrounds, offers the only effective way of improving their lives. A classic example of this strategy is the success the Communist Party had in the East End of London during the 1930s in undercutting the working class base Oswald Mosley's British Union of Fascists was building up in the area by combining the physical struggle against the fascists—above all, in the great Battle of Cable Street of 4 October 1936—with campaigns around material issues (notably rent) which won over many of the Mosleyite's supporters.[101] All this, however, merely highlights the fact that racism, and all the poverty, wretchedness and violence with which it is linked, flow from the nature of capitalist society. We have to remove the cause, as well as its symptoms.

Secondly, therefore, revolutionary socialists are committed to building a non-racial party of black and white workers which understands that racism can only be finally removed through the overthrow of the capitalist system. This strategy does not imply telling black people to wait for the socialist revolution. As we have seen, revolutionaries involve themselves fully in the daily battles against racism. But they do so understanding, not simply that racism has its roots in capitalism, but that capitalism itself can only be overthrown by a working class that has overcome its racial divisions and united against the common enemy. Revolutionary socialists are anti-racists not only because they despise racism for the moral obscenity that it is, but because a working class movement which does not confront racism will not be able to overthrow capital. The working class, as we have seen, is an international class: the spread of capitalism across the globe has created a proletariat that is itself spread across the globe and which has been formed by large scale immigration across national borders. Breaking down the racial barriers which this process helps erect between different groups of workers is a necessary condition of any successful socialist revolution.

Of course, this doesn't mean that racism will simply disappear once a socialist revolution has taken place. Marx pointed out that socialist society, 'as it emerges from capitalist society ... is thus in every respect, economically, morally and intellectually, still stamped with the birth-marks of the old society from whose womb it emerges.'[102] It would still be tainted with the filth of the past, including racism. Nevertheless, socialist revolution would strike racism a fatal blow. There are two reasons for this. First, as we have just seen, only a united working class could make the revolution in the first place. The revolutionary process would itself drastically weaken racial divisions. Second, the creation of a socialist society would, even in its earliest stages, involve dismantling the material structures of capitalism which are responsible for the existence of racism. Workers' revolution would thus be the beginning of a process which, over time, would make racism merely a bad memory. Socialist revolution and black liberation are inseparable.

From this perspective we can see why the charges that Marxism is 'Eurocentric' made by black radicals such as Cedric Robinson are mistaken. Marxism indeed emerged in Western Europe in response to the appearance of industrial capitalism, the capitalist mode of production in its developed form. At the centre of Marx's theory was his analysis of this unprecedented phenomenon. In the *Communist Manifesto* and the *Grundrisse* in particular he stresses capitalism's *universalising* role, the way in which it dragged humankind willy-nilly into the first genuinely global social system in history. Marx was clear sighted about the terrible suffering this entailed, especially for the peoples of what we now call the Third World: 'the extirpation, enslavement and entombment in mines of the indigenous population [of America]... the beginnings of the conquest and plunder of India, and the conversion of Africa into a preserve for the commercial hunting of black skins are all things which characterise the dawn of the era of capitalist production.'[103] But Marx argued that the emergence of the capitalist world system created the conditions of what he called 'human emancipation'—a revolution which in overthrowing capitalism would lay the basis of the abolition of class exploitation altogether and of all the other forms of oppression dividing and disabling humankind. Such a comprehensive emancipation was possible because capitalism rested on a universal class, the proletariat, a world class, formed from all the peoples of the globe, which could liberate itself only through an international revolution founded on the common interests of the exploited.

This conception of human emancipation informs the politics of the revolutionary Marxist tradition. It explains why, for example, the Communist International was, in the years immediately after the Russian Revolution of October 1917, the first socialist movement to see itself as a genuinely global movement which linked the struggle of the industrial working class to the anti-imperialist revolt of the colonial masses, whom Lenin and the Bolsheviks conceived as the subject of their own emancipation. It was the same vision of human emancipation which led CLR James to rally to the revolutionary socialist tradition—a commitment from which, whatever the peculiarities of his understanding of the tradition, he never thereafter flinched[104]—and which kept other radical black intellectuals like WEB Du Bois in a creative dialogue with Marxism. Even a version of this vision which had been debased by Stalinism allowed the Communist Party of the USA to build a significant base in Harlem during the 1930s (and to have an important influence on the riot of March 1935), despite fierce competition from black nationalists, notably followers of Marcus Garvey, and on the basis of an intransigent defence of the class unity of black and white workers.[105]

The great rebellions of black people, from the Haitian

Revolution to the Los Angeles rising are part of the revolutionary tradition which seeks to unite the movements for socialism and for black liberation. The struggle against racial oppression is an indispensable part of the revolutionary socialist project. Equally, however, without the victory of that project, the fight against racism cannot finally be won.

Notes

Notes

1. A Hacker, *Two Nations*, New York 1993, p. 3. The strength of Hacker's book is the mass of empirical evidence he amasses documenting the plight of black people in the US, both in the text and in 'Supplementary Tables' at the end of the book (pp. 225-36). For a critical assessment see D Roediger, 'The Racial Crisis of American Liberalism', *New Left Review*, 196, 1992. Whatever Hacker's failings, it is something of a scandal that the closest British equivalent to his book seems still to be D Smith, *Racial Disadvantage in Britain*, Harmondsworth, 1977, based on research conducted by Political and Economic Planning between 1972 and 1975.
2. See A Sivanandan, *Communities of Resistance*, London 1990, ch. 4, for a devastating critique of RAT.
3. An early example of 'socio-cultural pluralism' is Dilip Hiro's influential *Black British White British*, first published 1971: rev. edn., London 1992.
4. For a brief statement of the Marxist case, see A Callinicos, *The Fight against Racism*, London 1992.
5. A good example is the splendid polemic by Sivanandan, editor of the journal *Race and Class* and one of the most influential radical black intellectuals in Britain, against what he calls the 'Hokum of New Times', the capitulation to postmodernism that was virtually the last gasp of *Marxism Today*, now, happily, defunct: 'All that Melts into Air is Solid', reprinted in *Communities*.
6. C Robinson, *Black Marxism*, London 1983, pp. 2-3, 3-5.
7. Ibid., pp. 451, 244. There are other flaws in the book: its constipated academic style is no doubt connected to the mysticism mentioned in the text; Robinson's critique of historical materialism draws eclectically on ex-Marxist poseurs like Jean Baudrillard and Cornelius Castoriadis and anti-Marxist liberals like Shlomo Avinieri and Isaiah Berlin. Another radical black intellectual, Cornel West, writes much better and is at least quite open in espousing religious beliefs—what he calls 'Christian prophetic pragmatism': see

The American Evasion of Philosophy, London 1989, ch. 6. Robert Young offers a more philosophically sophisticated version of the critique of Marxism as Eurocentric in *White Mythologies*, London 1990.

8. Robinson, *Black Marxism*, p. 82.
9. M Marable, *How Capitalism Underdeveloped Black America*, Boston 1983, p. 260.
10. P Fryer, *Staying Power*, London 1984, pp. 165-90.
11. S Rose et al., *Not in Our Genes*, Harmondsworth 1984, pp. 126-7.
12. Z Bauman, *Modernity and the Holocaust*, Cambridge 1991, pp. 62-3, 65.
13. FM Snowden Jnr., *Blacks in Antiquity*, Cambridge Mass. 1970, pp. 182-3.
14. There is indeed much evidence especially of Asian influence during the archaic period (800-500 BC) which preceded the full flowering of classical Greece after the defeat of the Persian invasions at the beginning of the fifth century BC: see, for example, O Murray, *Archaic Greece*, London 1980. The weakness of Bernal's argument is that he concentrates on tracing Egyptian and Phoenician influences on individual practices and institutions—for example, the role of African and Asian colonisers in founding particular religious cults and cities, and the trace elements of Egyptian and Phoenician in the Greek language itself. What this misses out is the distinctive nature of classical Greek society as a totality, characterised by reliance on slave labour as the main source of ruling class income and the political institution of the city-state based on citizen armies of heavy infantry: see P Anderson, *Passages from Antiquity to Feudalism*, London 1974, GEM de Ste Croix, *The Class Struggle in the Ancient Greek World*, London 1981, and EM Wood, *Peasant-Citizen and Slave*, London 1988. Whatever the economic contacts, cultural influences and direct colonisations from outside which contributed to the emergence of classical Greece, it represented a different form of society from those which preceded and surrounded it in the Eastern Mediterranean.
15. M Bernal, *Black Athena*, I, London 1991, pp. 1-2.
16. Ibid., p. 1.
17. Herodotus, *The Histories*, Bk. II.
18. A Momigliano, *Alien Wisdom*, Cambridge 1975, p. 131.
19. J Herrin, *The Formation of Christendom*, Oxford 1987, p. 8.
20. H Arendt, *The Origins of Totalitarianism*, London 1986, p. 7.
21. Bauman, *Modernity*, p. 35. The tensions surrounding the Jews' position in pre-modern Europe were, in fact, closely

related to their peculiar economic position as often the main practitioners of commerce in predominantly agrarian societies: see A Leon, *The Jewish Question*, New York 1970, esp. chs. III and IV.

22. Arendt, *Origins*, p. 87.
23. Fryer, *Staying Power*, p. 134.
24. D Hume, *Essays, Moral, Political, and Literary*, Indianapolis 1985, pp. 629-30. Hume slightly toned down the racism of this passage in its final version: see ibid., p. 208 n. 10.
25. R Blackburn, *The Overthrow of Colonial Slavery 1776-1848*, London 1988, Introduction.
26. E Williams, *Capitalism and Slavery*, New York 1961, p. 6.
27. Blackburn, *Overthrow*, p. 11.
28. BJ Fields, 'Slavery, Race and Ideology in the United States of America', *New Left Review*, 181, 1990, p. 102.
29. Ibid., pp. 102-3.
30. Ibid., p. 105.
31. EM Wood, 'Capitalism and Human Emancipation', *New Left Review*, 167, 1988, p. 7.
32. Marx, *Capital*, I, Harmondsworth 1976, p. 899, and *Capital*, III, Moscow 1971, pp. 790-2.
33. Ibn Khaldûn, *The Muquaddimah*, 3 vols., New York 1958, I, pp. 80-1.
34. Marx, *Grundrisse*, Harmondsworth 1973, p. 507.
35. Marx, *Capital*, I, pp. 279-80.
36. Fields, 'Slavery', p. 114.
37. Fryer, *Staying Power*, p. 134.
38. See Chris Hitchens' interesting discussion of Kipling's role as the 'Bard of Empire' in *Blood, Class and Nostalgia*, London 1990, ch. 3.
39. Fryer, *Staying Power*, p. 190.
40. M Barker, *The New Racism*, London 1981. See also, for example, P Gilroy, *'There Ain't No Black in the Union Jack'*, London 1987, ch. 2.
41. See Rose et al., *Not in Our Genes* for criticism of these and related ideas.
42. A striking example is D Hiro's discussion of Afro-Caribbeans: see *Black British*, pp. 22-5.
43. The South African Marxist Neville Alexander develops an important critique of the concept of ethnicity in his book (written under the pseudonym No Sizwe) *One Azania One Nation*, London 1979.
44. EJ Hobsbawm, *The Age of Capital 1848-1875*, London 1977, p. 228; see generally ibid., ch. 11.
45. See S Castles and G Kosack, *Immigrant Workers and Class*

Structure in Western Europe, London 1973.
46. See J Rollo, 'Immigrant Workers in Western Europe', II, *International Socialism*, 1:97, 1977.
47. Marx and Engels, *Selected Correspondence*, Moscow 1965, pp. 236-7.
48. M Davis, *Prisoners of the American Dream*, London 1986, ch. 1.
49. P Foner, *Organized Labor and the Black Worker 1619-1981*, New York 1981, ch. 1. There are in fact further complications to the relationship between economic competition and racial divisions. For one thing, the economic and ethnic differences between groups of workers don't necessarily harden into full scale racial antagonisms: in the US, for example, the black-white divide has usually overriden other tensions. For another, the economic tensions don't have to be between different groups of workers: consider, for example, the clashes between Korean shopkeepers and the Latino poor during the LA rebellion.
50. WEB du Bois, *Black Reconstruction in America 1860-1880*, New York 1969, pp. 700-1. This explanation is capable of being misused. For an example, see D Roediger, *The Wages of Whiteness*, London 1991, and Paul D'Amato's critical review, 'US Rulers Divided Both to Conquer Each', *Socialist Worker*, Chicago November 1991.
51. See James's correspondence with Martin Glaberman, in P Buhle, ed., *CLR James: His Life and Work*, London 1988, pp. 153-63
52. Marx and Engels, *Collected Works*, London 1975-, III, p. 175.
53. B Anderson, *Imagined Communities*, London 1983, pp. 15-16. Anderson, however, stresses what he sees as the differences between nationalism and racism: 'The fact of the matter is that nationalism thinks in terms of historical destinies, while racism dreams of eternal contaminations, transmitted from the origins of time through an endless sequence of loathsome copulations: outside history.' (Ibid., p. 136). It is undoubtedly true that, as we have seen, racist ideology conceives race (or, more recently, ethnicity) as inescapable fate. Nevertheless, Anderson's argument fails to take into account the way in which in recent decades the idea of the national culture has become one of the main reasons used to justify, for example, tightening up immigration controls: consider, for example, Thatcher's infamous appeal to those afraid of being 'swamped by people with a different culture', discussed above. See also Gilroy, *'Ain't No Black'*, pp. 44ff.
54. EJ Hobsbawm, *The Age of Empire 1875-1914*, London 1987,

chs. 5 and 6.

55. See EO Wright et al., *Reconstructing Marxism*, London 1992, pp. 63-7, for a useful critique of the idea, put about by sociologists like Anthony Giddens, that explaining racism by the 'beneficial effects for capitalism' it has because of 'its consequences for working class disunity (divide and conquer)' is an untenable piece of 'functionalism'.
56. Robinson, *Black Marxism*, p. 451.
57. Gilroy, *'Ain't No Black'*, pp. 23-4.
58. Sivanandan, *Communities*, p. 52.
59. See the quotations from WEB du Bois, 'The African Roots of War' (1915), in Robinson, *Black Marxism*, pp. 334-5, n. 72.
60. R Ramdin, *The Making of the Black Working Class in Britain*, Aldershot 1987, p. 63.
61. See, for example, T Cliff, 'The Economic Roots of Reformism', in *Neither Washington Nor Moscow*, London 1982.
62. See M Kidron, 'Black Reformism', in *Capitalism and Theory*, London 1974.
63. A Callinicos, 'Marxism and Imperialism Today', *International Socialism*, 2:50, 1991, pp. 19-25.
64. Sivanandan, *Communities*, p. 181.
65. See J Baskin, *Striking Back*, Johannesburg 1991.
66. A Szymanski, 'Racial Discrimination and White Gain', *American Sociological Review*, 41, 1976, pp. 409-12.
67. Sivanandan, *Communities*, p. 29.
68. A Callinicos, *Against Postmodernism*, Cambridge 1989, ch. 5.
69. M Naylor and E Purdie, 'Results of the 1991 Labour Force Survey', *Employment Gazette*, April 1992, Tables 6 and 9.
70. EO Wright, *Classes*, London 1985, Table 6.4, p. 201. These figures should be taken as only indicative, since, because of flaws in Wright's theory of class, they almost certainly understate the size of the working class. See A Callinicos and C Harman, *The Changing Working Class*, London 1987, Appendix.
71. Hacker, *Two Nations*, pp. 232, 103. The figures for Britain are more mixed. According to a recent government survey, 39.2 percent of Afro-Caribbean workers are in unions, 34.2 percent of white workers, 30.2 percent of workers of Indian origin and 23.5 percent of those of Pakistani origin: *Financial Times*, 7 May 1993.
72. Sivanandan, *Communities*, pp. 51-8.
73. Gilroy, *'Ain't No Black'*, p. 247.
74. See A Shawki, 'Black Liberation and Socialism in the United States', *International Socialism*, 2:47, 1990, and K Ovenden,

Malcolm X: Socialism and Black Nationalism, London 1992.
75. Quoted in S Smith, 'Twilight of the American Dream', *International Socialism*, 2:54, 1992, pp. 20, 22.
76. *Forging a Black Community: Asian and Afro-Caribbean Struggles in Newham*, London 1991, p. 47.
77. M Davis, 'The Rebellion that Rocked a Superpower', *Socialist Review*, June 1992, p. 8.
78. What follows is heavily indebted to Davis, 'Rebellion', *Socialist Worker*, Chicago May and June 1992, D Hazen, ed., *Inside the LA Riots*, New York 1992 (hereinafter *ILAR*), and A Callinicos, 'The Meaning of the Los Angeles Riots', *Economic and Political Weekly*, 25 July 1992.
79. M Davis, *City of Quartz*, London 1990, ch. 5.
80. L Rodriguez, 'Deciphering LA Smoke Signals', in *ILAR*, p. 82.
81. Quoted in *Socialist Worker*, Chicago May 1992.
82. M Davis, 'Burning All Illusions in LA', in *ILAR*, p. 97.
83. See K Phillips, *The Politics of Rich and Poor*, New York 1991, and Smith, 'Twilight'.
84. P Kwong, 'The First Multicultural Riots', in *ILAR*, p. 88.
85. Ibid., pp. 90-1.
86. M Davis, 'Who Killed LA?', Isaac Deutscher Memorial Lecturer, London School of Economics, 29 April 1993.
87. Davis, 'Burning', p. 99.
88. M Marable, 'LA Point of View', in *ILAR*, p. 82.
89. L Sustar, 'The Fire Last Time', *Socialist Worker*, Chicago May 1992.
90. C Harman, 'The Summer of 1981: A Post-Riot Analysis', *International Socialism*, 2:14 1981, p. 14.
91. Hiro, *Black British*, p. 90.
92. Fryer, *Staying Power*, pp. 203-46.
93. See E Foner, *Reconstruction*, New York 1988, esp. ch. 7, and L Sustar, 'Racism and Class Struggle in the American Civil War Era', *International Socialism*, 2:55 1992.
94. Foner, *Organized Labor*, pp. 50, 66; see generally ibid., chs. 4-6.
95. *Forging a Black Community*, pp. 12, 28, 31, 41. 96. Ibid., p. 32.
97. Ibid., pp. 1, 48.
98. Gilroy, *'Ain't No Black'*, pp. 131, 133.
99. M Walker, *The National Front*, London 1977.
100. P Foot, 'David Widgery', *New Left Review*, 196 1992, p. 122. See more generally C Bambery, *Killing the Nazi Menace*, London 1992. It is sometimes claimed that it was not the ANL, but rather Thatcher, with her appeal to white fears of

being 'swamped by people with a different culture', who killed off the Nazis, by stealing their clothes. This isn't an especially plausible explanation. For one thing, the Tories were relatively cautious about mounting any full scale offensive against black people after 1979, and especially after the 1981 riots (only in the last two or three years have there been signs of the Tories wishing to make serious use of race and immigration as issues). In any case, as the French case discussed in the text shows, official racism tends to strengthen the fascists by giving them confidence and their ideas greater legitimacy. This certainly was the pattern in Britain in the 1960s and 1970s: see Paul Foot's classic study *Immigration and Race in British Politics*, Harmondsworth 1965.

101. P Piratin, *Our Flag Stays Red*, London 1978, ch. 3.
102. Marx and Engels, *Collected Works*, 1975-, XXIV, p. 85.
103. Marx, *Capital*, I, p. 915.
104. See A Callinicos, *Trotskyism*, Milton Keynes 1990, pp. 61-6, and Shawki, 'Black Liberation', pp. 58-68.
105. M Naison, *Communists in Harlem during the Depression*, New York 1983, esp. Part I.

Index

Index

Other publications from Bookmarks

Fighting racism

Malcolm X: Socialism and Black Nationalism
Kevin Ovenden
A best seller, unravelling the life of Malcolm X against the turbulent background of the US in the 1950s and 1960s. A critical examination of what Malcolm X offers the struggle today.
£2.95, 96pp

The Ghetto Fights
Marek Edelman
First hand account of the inspiring struggle against the Nazis in the war-time Warsaw ghetto.
£3.95, 120pp

Fascism, Stalinism and the United Front
Leon Trotsky
A strategy for stopping the Nazis. Ignored tragically in the 1930s, invaluable for today.
£4.95, 288pp

Killing the Nazi Menace
Chris Bambery
How to fight the fascists—drawn from the experience of the 1930s and the 1970s.
£1.50, 48pp

Guides to socialism

How Marxism Works
Chris Harman
An outstanding explanation of the main themes of Marxist thought.
£2.50, 96pp

The Revolutionary Ideas of Karl Marx
Alex Callinicos
Over a century since Marx analysed capitalism as a system prone to recession and wars, this book shows his ideas to be as relevant today.
£3.95, 208pp

Arguments for revolutionary socialism
John Molyneux
Any socialist faces a barrage of questions, from human nature to overpopulation. This is an invaluable guide to the answers.
£3.50, 128pp

The Changing Working Class
Alex Callinicos and Chris Harman
Are today's white collar workers really middle class? Has the traditional manual working class disappeared? What about the 'underclass'?
£3.95, 106pp

What is the real Marxist Tradition?
John Molyneux
Explodes the myth that social democracy and Stalinism have anything to do with socialism and searches for the genuine tradition.
£2.50, 80pp

Socialism: Utopian and Scientific
Frederick Engels
Still one of the best short guides to what the struggle for socialism is really all about.
Engels links the fight for the future to the shape of the present society. In doing so he builds a stable bridge that links our hopes and endeavours of today with the struggle for a better world.
£2.95, 128pp

Political Theory

Crime, Class and Corruption: the Politics of the Police
Audrey Farrell
This examination of the real roots of crime finds the police have no role in stopping it, and instead hold up a system that gives rise to crime in the first place.
£5.95, 208pp

Marxism and the Trade Union Struggle: the General Strike of 1926
Tony Cliff and Donny Gluckstein
In the light cast by the greatest ever strike in Britain, the treachery of the trade union leaders casts a clear cut shadow.
£6.95, 320pp

Sexual Politics

Sex, Class and Socialism
Lindsey German
Women now have far greater control over their lives than ever before, yet their oppression persists. Lindsey German analyses how the family shapes women's lives under capitalism.
£5.95, 256pp

Abortion: A woman's right to choose
Ruth Brown
The whys and hows of fighting for abortion rights.
£2.00, 40pp

Ireland

Ireland's Permanent Revolution
Chris Bambery
The starting point of this book, now in its third edition, is that Britain created the mess in Ireland and should therefore get out now. But it goes further than this and argues for a strategy to unite workers North and South in a struggle to get rid of the border and fight for socialism.
£3.50, 128pp

Labour in Irish History
James Connolly
An outstanding historical analysis of the struggle for Irish freedom. Still astonishingly relevant today.
£2.95, 160pp

Culture

Red Shelley
Paul Foot
An outcast in his own time—an athiest, a socialist, a republican and a supporter of women's rights—Shelley has been abused and sanitised by the establishment as a 'romantic'. This book sets the record straight.
£4.95, 288pp

Shelley's Revolutionary Year
Paul Foot
The great writings inspired by the 1819 Peterloo massacre.
A Redwords book
£3.95, 122pp

Literature and Revolution
Leon Trotsky
The first British edition of this outstanding analysis of the relationship between art and society.
A Redwords book
£7.95, 284pp

International

The Lost Revolution: Germany 1919-23
Chris Harman
The mass working class upheavals that swept Germany after the first world war shaped the world we live in as radically as any event this century—for the loss of this revolution opened the door to both Hitler and Stalin.
£5.95, 336pp

The Fire Last Time: 1968 and After
Chris Harman
The year which rocked rulers from Paris to Prague, Berkeley to Berlin. Why the explosion occurred and how it eventually fizzled out.
£6.95, 416pp

Nicaragua: What went wrong
Mike Gonzalez
Traces the road from the Sandinista's 1979 insurrection to electoral defeat in 1990.
£4.50, 144pp

The Road to Tiananmen Square
Charlie Hore
What the 1949 revolution was really all about, and the thrilling story of the new, workers' revolution which nearly broke out in 1989.
£4.95, 160pp

Israel: the Hijack State
John Rose
The origins of Zionism, its significance to imperialism and the resistance it has sparked.
£2.50, 80pp

Intifada: Zionism, Imperialism and Palestinian Resistance.
Phil Marshall
An analysis of the struggle that refuses to die.
£5.95, 256pp

South Africa between Apartheid and Capitalism
Alex Callinicos
Interviews with leading figures on the South African left, compiled as the country stands at the crossroads.
£5.95, 192pp

South Africa between Reform and Revolution
Alex Callinicos
A brilliant and unique analysis of the forces fighting to shape the future of South Africa.
£4.95, 242pp

265 Seven Sisters Road, London N4 2DE
PO Box 16085, Chicago, Il. 60616
GPO Box 1473N, Melbourne 3001